GERRARD WINSTANLEY
and the republic of heaven

by David Boulton

Dales Historical Monographs

Published by
Dales Historical Monographs, Hobsons Farm, Dent,
Cumbria LA10 5RF, UK.
Tel/Fax 015396 25321

ISBN 0-9511578-4-1

Typesetting by Dales Historical Monographs
Printed by
Stramongate Press, Aynam Mills, Little Aynam, Kendal,
Cumbria LA9 7AH

This book is printed on recycled paper

Front Cover: David Blackburn's *"Three"* (1998)
(private collection) reproduced by kind permission of the artist and
Hart Gallery, 113 Upper Street, Islington, London N1 1QN.

__David Boulton__ joined the staff of Tribune under Michael Foot in 1959 and subsequently edited Sanity, the newspaper of the Campaign for Nuclear Disarmament. He was a founder member with Donald Soper of the Christian Socialist Movement. Recruited by Sidney Bernstein to Granada Television in 1966, he became Editor of World in Action and Head of News, Current Affairs and Arts. His broadcasting awards include the Royal Television Society's Cyril Bennett Award "for creative services to television". He was appointed a member of the Broadcasting Complaints Commission in 1996 and its successor body, the Broadcasting Standards Commission, in 1997. He represents the Commission on the British and Irish Ombudsman Association.

His nine books include studies of conscientious objection in the First World War, Protestant private armies in modern Ulster, and the Lockheed bribery scandal. His most recent book, with his wife Anthea, is "In Fox's Footsteps", a revisionist study of the Quaker leader George Fox, and his most recent pamphlet is "The Faith of a Quaker Humanist". He edits "Sea of Faith", the quarterly magazine of the Sea of Faith Network which "explores and promotes religious faith as a human creation", and he runs Dales Historical Monographs from his home in Dent, Cumbria, publishing work on local and Quaker history.

Acknowledgments

My grateful thanks to Michael Foot, who first contributed a Foreword to a book of mine some forty years ago and was kind enough to agree a second time following his inspirational talk on Winstanley in Walton church on the 350th anniversary of the George's Hill dig; to David Blackburn, whose visionary landscape paintings are making their own inspirational contribution to contemporary art, for permission to reproduce his pastel *Three* as a front cover; to sculptor Andrew Whittle for the photographs of his Winstanley monument, intended for George's Hill (where it is pictured) pending the agreement of local residents, not all of whom are wildly enthusiastic about the earth (including their exclusive golf course) being made a common treasury; to Sheila Noble, my one-time *Tribune* colleague and all-time friend and critic, for overcoming her distaste for all this religious language and subjecting my text to her formidable copy-editing techniques (though remaining howlers are my responsibility); to Anthea Boulton for her wise suggestions and stealthy revisions; and to those of my Quaker and Sea of Faith readers who encouraged me to fit this study into a busy life - particularly those who, by placing advance orders, made it impossible for me to abandon GW in the depths of the seventeenth century, which a growing awareness of my own limitations sometimes tempted me to do.

CONTENTS

FOREWORD
by Michael Foot

Gerrard Winstanley wrote his twenty books and pamphlets within a four-year period. But these four years, 1648 to 1651, saw the kingdom of England become a republic, and it was Winstanley's visionary hope that the republic would in turn become a "common-wealth", a "common treasury", or what David Boulton calls here "the republic of heaven".

Not content to hope and dream, Winstanley acted. He led his band of True Levellers on to England's commons and claimed them for the common people. For three and a half centuries his astonishing achievement in creating his experimental community, and sustaining it for twelve months despite the brutal attacks of church and state establishment, continued to inspire successive generations of radicals, chartists and socialists of every hue. Winstanley famously insisted that "action is the life of all", that the spade was mightier than the word, but it is his words which have survived to tell us of his deeds.

And what words! Winstanley was an inspired writer and, if there were such a thing as a sacred canon of radical English literature, Winstanley's works would be there, not far behind those of Milton, Byron, Shelley, Hazlitt and William Morris. David Boulton is right to tell Winstanley's story, wherever possible, in his own vivid words. They are seventeenth century words, making free with the biblical language that saturated seventeenth century England; but they speak no less eloquently to our condition at the end of the twentieth century. The language of political discourse has changed, and Tony Blair's world is not Oliver Cromwell's. But David Boulton's study demonstrates that the True Leveller's vision, what he calls Winstanley's "enabling dream", is not fixed and confined in a romantic past but remains relevant today, despite all the convulsive changes of the intervening centuries.

Revolutions have come and gone, walls have gone up and come down, but the dream of Winstanley's republic of heaven endures. His visionary but practical millenarianism has a vital contribution to make as we enter our own new millennium, and David Boulton, true to his *Tribune* roots, has done us a service in demonstrating that Winstanley is no less relevant in post-modernity than he was in the early-modern world of the British revolution.

House of Commons, October 1999

Preface

Gerrard Winstanley has been much studied and written about, not least in this the 350th anniversary year of his dig at George's Hill. But much of what has been written sits in academic journals, accessible enough to the determined scholar, less so to the general reader. So my main aim has been to provide a short, inexpensive, readable account of Winstanley's work: his words, his actions and his life. I doubt that anyone on the academic Winstanley circuit will find here any fact of which they were completely ignorant, though they may find some new slants on familiar themes. The general reader, on the other hand, if I succeed in reaching her, can anticipate an extraordinary tale of vision, idealism, action and endurance, which is the story of no less an event than the birth of democratic socialism and the dawn of religious humanism.

Winstanley is often quoted by socialist writers. The simplicity and passionate eloquence of his writing style makes him a wonderful quarry for epigraphs. But he is less often quoted in context, and with Winstanley context is the life of all. So I take the reader through his twenty works one by one, chronologically, because that is the only way to make proper sense of them. Virtually every one of his pamphlets and books is precipitated by a specific event, at what was surely the most eventful time in English history. Between 1648 when his first work appeared, and 1652 when his last went to press, the pace of events in revolutionary England was such that neither those who participated in them nor historians who look back on them ever managed to agree on what was going on. In four years England moved from a notional monarchy at war with itself to a *de facto* republic with a deposed king, to a republic with no king, to various forms of "Commonwealth" heading for military dictatorship. It lost in turn Church, Lords and Crown. It tottered towards revolution and teetered away from it. Winstanley's work can only be properly understood in direct relation to changing events, and if I have done nothing else I have presented him in that context.

Much of this book is beautifully written, because I have used Winstanley's own words at every opportunity. My principal source has been Sabine's *Works* and, with Sabine, I have preserved Winstanley's spelling, punctuation and capitalisation, though not always his italics. For *Englands Spirit Unfoulded*, the one work discovered since Sabine, I have followed Aylmer's text as produced in *Past and Present*. The many other sources cited are the best indication I can give of my indebtedness to Winstanley scholars, and students wishing to pursue their own Winstanley studies could not make a better start than with the works of Christopher Hill, Andrew Bradstock, and the others listed in the text or source notes - to which I would wish to add David W Petegorsky's pioneering (1940) *Left-Wing Democracy in the English Civil War*. From each of them I have learned a great deal (even if, occasionally, I dare to disagree on points of interpretation).

After taking my readers through Winstanley's words and deeds, I turn to the thorny old question of Winstanley's relationship to the Quakers. I cannot claim to have turned up any new factual evidence of direct contact to add to the important discoveries of Barry Reay and James Alsop, but again, by close attention to the changing dynamics of both Winstanley's post-Digger life and early Quakerism, I hope to have cast more light on the problem. We know that Winstanley's life followed a puzzling trajectory after 1652, but researchers have not always appreciated that Quakerism too was far from static, passing rapidly through political and non-political phases, sometimes adopting a loyalist stance (one of "critical engagement") towards Cromwell's regime and the Army, sometimes an oppositionist and prophetic position - and sometimes both at once. It is only by understanding these dynamics that we can hope to make some sense of the Winstanley-Quaker relationship, by which we may hope for a better understanding of both Winstanley's small and short-lived True Leveller communities and Fox's far larger and more permanent movement.

Finally I attempt the really difficult questions: what has the Christian communist Winstanley to say to us in a post-Christian and post-communist age? What is the relevance of this early-modern thinker to our own post-modern times? Not all my readers will find my answers satisfying particularly those who reject all these "posts-". But I offer them as a contribution to the Winstanley discussion, which will not go away.

David Boulton
Dent, October 1999

I
The making of a revolutionary

What on earth *was* Gerrard Winstanley? A utopian communist dreamer? All three of these words may be questioned, though there was certainly a utopian element to his project, it clearly focused on common ownership, and his single most important insight came to him, he tells us, in a "trance". He has been called a seventeenth century Marxist, but that's like calling Moses (who preached love of one's neighbour long before Jesus of Nazareth) a seventh century BCE Christian. He has been claimed (absurdly) for orthodox Christianity, for liberation theology, for socialism, anarchism, atheism, rationalism, secularism, humanism, communitarianism - even the Third Way. "A mystical humanistic Christian pantheist" is one scholar's shot at categorisation[1], and that's leaving out the communism. Quakers who like him have tried to prove he was a Quaker, Quakers who don't like him have tried to prove he wasn't. Whatever else he was and wasn't, though, he was a revolutionary: a radical in the root sense of the word, one who (in his case literally) dug down to the root causes of the poverty, inequality and alienation he saw all about him in an England torn apart by a civil war conducted on both sides in the name of a God he had come to believe was the very devil.

In one sense his appearance on the stage of history was little more than a walk-on walk-off part. He had his entrance and his exit, and the one was closely followed by the other. The whole of Winstanley's known work - twenty pamphlets[2], not to mention what he wrote on the soil with his spade - was published and enacted within a four year period. His ministry was almost as brief as that of Jesus, who lasted barely three years before he was killed off. Winstanley wasn't killed off: he retired hurt. But he has been resurrected several times since. However dull and respectable Quakerism became, it never quite shook off his influence. Whether the Christian Communist tendency in the French revolution or William Blake in England ever read Winstanley I do not know, but they were heirs to his tradition. I attach no mystical significance to the fact that the Communist Manifesto was published exactly 200 years after Winstanley's first stride into print, but both nineteenth and twentieth century Marxists were quick to claim and canonise him, even if they had to clean him up first by scraping off what they thought were the embarrassing encrustations of his theological language. When state communism on the Marxist-Leninist-Stalinist model was seen to have gone horribly wrong, Winstanley was paraded once again as a guide to how it might have been, and perhaps might yet be. The collapse of communism and our current postmodern suspicion of all isms might have been expected to allow the old Digger a decent burial. But no! On the three hundred and fiftieth anniversary of the day Winstanley's spade disturbed the sod of George's Hill, near Walton-on-Thames, a new generation of Diggers proclaiming "The Land is Ours" showed that Christ (in the metaphorical and revolutionary sense in which Winstanley used the term) still makes the occasional attempt to rise in sons and daughters.

Any attempt at a biography of Winstanley the man, as distinct from a study of Winstanley the pamphlets, has to be an exercise in building bricks with little straw and not much sand, or constructing a jigsaw with all but a random handful of its pieces missing. It is generally assumed, for lack of other evidence, that the "Garrard, son of Winstanlie" whose baptism is recorded in the Wigan parish register in 1609 is our man, especially as the pamphleteer refers to his Lancashire background in his first publication. His father, Edward, is described in the register as a mercer, or textile-dealer, and he may or may not be the same Edward who was a burgess of Wigan at his death in 1639, when he was described as "Mr", suggesting that the family had some social standing. The fact that an Edmund Winstanley and his wife were presented to the church courts in 1605 for holding conventicles - illegal "nonconformist" meetings - has been seized on as evidence of a long tradition of dissent within the family, but there is no clear evidence linking Edmund to Edward, let alone to Gerrard, and Winstanley was a not uncommon name in the Wigan area (where the family name is derived from the nearby village of Winstanley). In any case, the charge against Edmund and his wife was dismissed, which leaves us with nothing more than an unproven suspicion of some unspecified unorthodoxy. Moreover, Edmund's conventicle could as easily have been Catholic as protestant non-conformist. There is not enough here on which to build a convincing radical pedigree.

Winstanley's fluent and strikingly original writing style indicates that he received an education of some sort, though he scarcely ever refers to other books (apart from the Bible), and does not write like an academic. On at least one occasion he quotes Latin, which has suggested to some that he had attended grammar school. (There was a Free Grammar School in Wigan from 1596, and another in nearby Upholland[3]). He is scornful of universities, the breeding grounds of hireling priests, and generally dismissive of formal education. But we know nothing of the education he received in the 1620s.

In or shortly before 1630, at the age of 20 or 21 if his baptism entry has been correctly identified, he left Lancashire for London to be apprenticed in the cloth trade. His "master", somewhat unusually, was a woman, Sarah Gates, and the Canadian scholar James Alsop has suggested[4] that Winstanley may have been a distant kinsman. Sarah Gates was the widow of a former Puritan minister turned cloth merchant, and as well as taking on her husband's business she also inherited his well-stocked theological library. Despite his later disdain of book learning, we may reasonably guess that the young apprentice picked up more than trade knowledge from his employer, in whose household he probably lodged.

In 1637, on completion of his indentures, Gerrard became a freeman of the Merchant Taylors Company, probably financing his business on credit - the usual way of starting out on one's own. On 28 September 1640 he married Susan King, daughter of a small landowner in Surrey. But owing to either the general disruption of London trade caused by the outbreak of civil war in 1642 or to his own lack of commercial ability, his business failed in 1643. He describes in *A Watchword to the City of London and the Armie* (1649) how "I was beaten out both of estate and trade, and forced to accept of the good will of friends crediting of me, to live a Countrey-life, and there likewise by the burthen of Taxes and much Free-quarter [the system by which soldiers were billeted on householders who were required to feed and house them without payment], my weak back found the burthen heavier than I could bear". In 1660, after the Restoration, he was sued by creditors, and acknowledged that "in the year of the Lord 1643 when the late unhappie wars in England were violent, your oratour left off his trading... by reason of the badness of times".

Winstanley did not return to Wigan, perhaps because the town was fiercely royalist, whereas he was decidedly parliamentarian, having subscribed to the Solemn League and Covenant in 1643. Instead, the "Countrey-life" to which he was forced to retreat was apparently lived at or near Cobham, Surrey, on or near his father-in-law's property. The King family may have given him employment as a cowherd and a roof over his head before he turned again to self-employment as a grazier, renting or leasing and perhaps buying land on credit on which to graze his neighbours' cattle. Soon after his move, he was evidently identifying himself with religious and political dissent (since the two went hand in glove). In Wigan, it seems, and perhaps at first in London, he had been an orthodox attender at parish church, since he tells us in *The New Law of Righteousnes* that he was formerly "a blind professor [one who professed religion] and strict goer to church... and a hearer of sermons". At that time he "believed as the learned clergy... believed". Subsequently he had "gon through the ordinance of dipping" [5], which is to say he had joined a Baptist congregation. Baptism in turn was soon rejected. This was a standard trajectory for those whom the revolution and civil war radicalised: from Puritan conformist to Puritan nonconformist, to membership of a break-away church, to free-wheeling "seeking" and outright opposition to institutional religion, often by "Ranting" or, a few years later, "Quaking". Among Winstanley's associates at this time was the radical John Fielder in nearby Kingston, who would soon turn to Quakerism as the continuing expression of his agitation.

It seems very likely that one spur to radicalism was Winstanley's direct experience of poverty. The winter of 1647/8 was unusually bitter, following a failed harvest, and there were huge increases in the Army levy in Surrey and the home counties. These, along with forced free-quarter, fell most heavily on the poorest who lacked the means or clout to avoid them. In *The Saints Paradice* (probably 1648) he lists some of the economic disasters he had seen, and perhaps experienced at first hand: "losses of his estate by fire, water, being cheated by false-spirited men, death of his cattle, or many such like casualties, whereby he becomes poor... and meets with hard language, hungry belly, to be despised, imprisoned". Such calamity and humiliation would have been felt all the more by the son of an esquire - a "Mr" - and a once-self-employed man who had been something in the City. In 1648, as the civil war entered its second and decisive phase, Gerrard Winstanley took up his pen and started writing.

II
The "sea of truth" and the radical underground

Early in 1648 Winstanley delivered to Giles Calvert's printing shop at the Black-Spread-Eagle, West End of "Pauls" (the "St" is ostentatiously dropped, as the radicals refused to recognise Romish canonisation) the manuscript of a pamphlet called *The Mysterie of God, Concerning the Whole Creation, Mankinde*. This was quickly followed by another, *The Breaking of the Day of God*, for which we have a precise publication date: May 20 1648. A third pamphlet, *The Saints Paradice*, apparently dating from the summer, was printed by Calvert before the end of the year. Calvert's press requires its own historian. Throughout the war years in the forties, the republic in the fifties, and on into the Restoration sixties till his death in 1663, this intrepid pioneer of "publish and be damned" issued a stream of radical literature: Leveller, True Leveller, Ranter and Quaker. After 1663 his widow would carry on the work in defiance of the restored king and established church [6].

The Mysterie is dedicated to "my beloved countrymen of the county of Lancaster", though whether this first edition ever reached Wigan we cannot tell. Winstanley recognises that his old friends in the north, and probably his new acquaintances in the south, might wonder at the temerity of a working man like himself claiming to explain so large a matter as God's mystery, for he says "Do not be surprised to see my name here, for God does not always choose the learned in whom to manifest himself". What he has to say he knows "first, by my own experience", and only secondarily by scripture. This is contrasted with the book-learning of the educated clergy. "He that preaches from the book and not from the annointing is no true minister but a hireling that preaches only to get a temporary living. Some old professors, and book-hirelings especially, are offended and brand the Saints as men full of errors. But you must be dead to your customs before you can run into the sea of truth."

This insistence - a continuing refrain in Winstanley, and soon to be repeated even more forcefully by George Fox and the early Quakers - that knowledge comes by direct inward experience rather than through the authority of books and the wise and learned, had its roots, paradoxically, in the authority of scripture. *Jeremiah* (31: 33-4) had prophesied that God would make a new covenant with his people in which his law would be written "in their hearts... And they shall teach no more every man his neighbour, and every man his brother, saying, Know the Lord: for they shall all know me, from the least of them unto the greatest". Winstanley and the radicals with whom he was keeping company by the late 1640s saw the new covenant as starting in their own revolutionary times. What need of clergy when men would "no more teach every man his neighbour", or of books when the law would be written in men's hearts? The only true teacher was the inward teacher, the Christ experienced as having come to "teach his people himself".

The "mysterie" Winstanley expounds in his first venture into print is that, contrary to what the Calvinist clergy teach, God will "redeem not part but all mankind from death". "In the end every man shall be saved, though some at the last hour". "Even the lost, who were cast into the fire, shall receive mercy and the whole of mankind shall be delivered from the curse." The "Serpent" is to be understood as man's selfishness - an identification Winstanley continues to make throughout his writings. Selfishness, and all its evil consequences, are to be destroyed by God, "and when his work is completed, he will dwell in the whole creation, in every man and woman without exception". Winstanley then draws on the book of *Revelation* to argue that God's seven dispensations of history are coming to an end. "In this age also the rage of the Serpent increases. To me it appears very plain that the great bitterness and reproaches now heaped on those called sectaries is the beginning of the beast's sorrow". The Serpent - selfishness - is about to be cast into the lake of fire, and an age of universal unselfishness will begin. "It quiets the heart to know that, whatsoever befalls, it is God's dispensation and that in his own time he will bring it to a good issue".

There are two doctrines here which were deeply subversive to orthodoxy and authority. The first is the challenge to the contemporary orthodoxy of Calvinism: the belief that a few are predestined by God to salvation and the many to damnation. The second is the suggestion that it is the unlearned and the "sectaries" - those who had separated themselves from the national church - who would be God's agents in bringing in the kingdom of God: an exact reversal of what the churches taught. And it was the *social order* itself, not just its current theological gloss, which was being subverted. The clergy and men of property tended to the view that *they* were God's elect to whom the kingdom was entrusted. Why else had God rewarded them with riches and power and honour, if not as a sign of their election? If all were to be saved, what price social distinction? If the despised sectaries, common trouble-makers all, were the heralds of the seventh dispensation which would see God's rule on earth, presumably through them, where did that leave the masters of property? Undone and dispossessed? Universalism was a levelling doctrine, and to privilege sectaries was to turn the world upside down.

How new and original was all this? Winstanley's *Mysterie* has been credited as the first fully universalist polemic, going far beyond the current Arminian critique of Calvinism which, while rejecting predestination in the name of free will, thereby allowed that some would be damned as a consequence of their own choice. More than a century would pass before universalism would begin to make an appearance in any of the organised churches. In this, then, Winstanley was a theological pioneer, ahead even of his most radical contemporaries, even if the historians of theology have not as yet given him his due.

The doctrine that it was the poor despised sectaries rather than the men of learning, wealth and power who would lead the way to the kingdom was less novel, if not less subversive. Here the 1648 Winstanley was expressing ideas which, in one form or another, were already exciting radicals around the country. These ideas had a long but long-supressed history. Since Christianity had begun as a religion of the poor and oppressed, expressing from the start a longing for the day when the proud would be scattered, the mighty put down from their seats, those of low degree exalted, the hungry filled and the rich sent empty away, a radical tendency was built into the deep foundations of the church as a permanent embarrassment to the proud, the rich and the mighty who ran it for their own purposes and had no intention whatever of being put down from their seats. This radicalism, expressed theologically but social in its concrete application, was liable to break surface in times of tension, trouble and dislocation.

Joachim of Fiore, Italy, in the twelfth century, famously taught that history was divided into a trinity of ages: that of the Father (the Old Testament period), that of the Son (from Christ to his own day) and that of the Spirit, which was imminent (Joachim made the naive miscalculation of dating it precisely to 1260, based on a mystical reading of *Revelation*). The Spirit would usher in a golden age in which men were ruled not by the law, as in the age of the Father, nor by the church, as in the age of the Son, but by the spirit of truth within their hearts. Commonality of goods, hitherto confined to the monastery as the prototype of paradise, would henceforth embrace all mankind. Joachim's "Everlasting Gospel", spread by his own order and perhaps by fringes of the Cistercian movement, became a rallying cry for radicals and the marginalised across Europe and into England. The fourteenth century mystic Richard Rolle of Yorkshire, clearly influenced by the Joachim tradition, taught the ultimate unity of God and man (at least the spiritual man). They were as inseparable, he wrote, as coal and fire, the air and light, wool and the dye in which it is dipped. Rolle attacked the system by which the church taxed the poor by tithes, and accused "the under-officers at courts... and the King's ministers" of corruption and the nobles of extortion[2].

Rolle also seems to allude to a day when theft would no longer be a problem, "when all property is held in common". Communism seems to have been at the heart of the preaching of another turbulent Yorkshireman (at least, he began his career as a priest in York) later in the fourteenth century. John Ball was excommunicated in 1366 for his seditious preaching and jailed in Maidstone. In 1381 he was rescued by the Kentish rebels who made him their spiritual leader as they marched on London in the Peasants' Revolt. At Blackheath he preached on the already popular text, "Whan Adam dalf and Eve span, Wo was thanne a gentilman?" It was no rhetorical question to John Ball and his followers. In Eden, when Adam delved the soil for food and Eve spun the thread for clothing, there were no gentry: so it would be when Paradise was regained. The gentry, however, saw things a little differently and accused him, perhaps correctly, of urging the killing of all lords and prelates. John Ball was hanged, but his memory and message, as expressed in an inspired couplet, lingered on, particularly on the more radical fringes of the proto-Protestant Lollard movement, led by yet another rebel Yorkshireman, John Wycliffe, which so plagued the church through the fifteenth century till the Reformation.

Wycliffe's teachings spread to the continent where, allied with those of Jan Hus in Bohemia, they laid the foundations of the "Radical Reformation". By 1520 Thomas Muntzer in Germany is complaining to Luther that the clergy have "seduced the church of God", being hypocrites who promote not the faith "but their own insatiable avarice". The church was led not by God's clergy but by "hell-grounded priests". When attempts were made by the rulers temporal and spiritual to rid themselves of this turbulent agitator, Muntzer organised his growing flock "with the intention of bringing the people together with a common purpose of overthrowing the wicked and preparing the way for God's final transformation of the world"[3]. In his *Vindication and Refutation*, written at the height of the peasants' war in 1525, Muntzer asks:

"What is the evil brew from which all usury, theft and robbery springs but the assumption of our lords and princes that all creatures are their property? The fish in the water, the birds in the air, the plants on the face of the earth - it all has to belong to them!... To add insult to injury, they have God's commandment proclaimed to the poor: God has commanded that you should not steal. But it avails them nothing. For while they do violence to everyone, flay and fleece the poor farm worker, tradesman and everything that breathes... yet should any of the latter commit the pettiest crime, he must hang... It is the lords themselves who make the poor man their enemy. If they refuse to do away with the cause of insurrection how can trouble be avoided in the long run? If saying that makes me an inciter to insurrection, so be it!" [4].

Sure of God's support, Muntzer led his followers into battle against the "hell-grounded" priests and princes. They sacked abbeys, plundered nunneries, pillaged monasteries and looted castles and noble houses. Why not, since these belonged to the devil? Pledged to destroy private property, they marched on property's defenders - but God failed to keep his appointment with Muntzer's destiny. Six thousand were killed, and Muntzer was captured and beheaded. Luther's princes and prelates saved the day for their own God: the god of property. Muntzer was denounced as a monster and his "communist" allies were excoriated as antichrist, an awful warning of the consequences of rebellion against God's anointed ministers in church and state. Yet the radical tradition of the "Everlasting Gospel", of the cry of the oppressed, was not so easily despatched. In the century between Muntzer and Winstanley it made its occasional forays from the underground, to the continuing unease of the mighty in their seats.

The religious and social doctrines of the "Radical Reformation" were carried to London by refugees from the continent. "Anabaptists" were first recorded in the city's independent churches, tolerated so long as they remained congregations of foreign exiles, as early as the 1540s. But it was a Dutch mystic rather than the disciples of Munster whose ideas took firmest root among the English radical underground. Hendrick Niclaes was born in or about 1502. By the 1540s his followers were calling themselves "the Family of Love". "H.N", as he signed his works, taught that the Bible was a collection of allegories and that heaven and hell were human states on earth. The Puritan preacher John Knewstub, in *A Confutation of Monstrous and Horrible Heresies taught by H.N.* (1579) complained that "H.N. turns religion upside down. He buildeth heaven here upon earth; he maketh God man and man God" [5]. Between 1573 and 1575 no fewer than eighteen of his books were translated into English, and the Family pursued its obscure underground existence for another century. Sometimes persecuted (and it is from the charges they faced that we can piece together something of their beliefs and practices), sometimes protected by court sympathisers, Family groups seem to have operated not so much as a separatist sect but as secret cells within the official Church. Some parish churches and chapelries, such as that at Grindleton, at the foot of Pendle Hill, Lancashire, became publicly identified with Familist views. In 1617 the curate Roger Brierley and his congregation faced fifty heresy charges, including the doctrine that "a motion rising from the spirit is more to be rested in than the Word itself" and that "a man having the spirit may read, pray or preach without any other calling whatsoever". Brierley later moved to Kildwick, over the Yorkshire border, and his Familist successor there, John Webster, became a chaplain in the New Model Army. Niclaes's works were again reprinted and widely circulated when censorship collapsed in the 1640s, and William Penn at the end of the century, in his preface to Fox's *Journal*, acknowledged direct Familist influence on early Quakerism. In the 1680s one of the last surviving Familist groups referred to its members as "a sort of refined Quakers" [6].

The earliest English Familists were described as mainly "cowherds, clothiers and such-like mean people". It was the tendency of radical doctrine to privilege and empower just such people, the poor, which was so unsettling for the rich. As church and state censors lost their grip after 1642, the "mean people" found their voice in the now openly declared heresies of the gathered churches. Bruno Ryves complained that the lower classes of Chelmsford were saying out loud that kings were burdens, the master-servant relationship had no ground in the New Testament, there was neither bond nor free in Christ, ranks such as the gentry and peerage were "heathenish distinctions", there was no ground in nature or scripture why one man should have £1000 per annum and another not £1, that gentlemen should be made to work for their living or else should not eat, that it were a happy thing if there were no universities and no books but the Bible, and that a congregation should be free to choose any gifted man as minister. By the mid-forties, radical Baptists were refusing "hat honour", "theeing" and "thouing" their social betters as if they were mere equals, and emphasising the superiority of the "inward light" and direct inspiration over the academic wisdom of their superiors.

Leveller Richard Overton could write in 1647: "I am confident that it must be the poor, the simple and mean things of this earth that must confound the mighty and the strong", and in the same year representatives of the Army rank and file famously claimed that "the poorest man in England" had as good a right as the richest to participate in choosing his member of the House of Commons. When Winstanley insists, first, that the poor will be saved, then that they have as natural a right to experiential knowledge as their betters, and finally (in *A Watch-Word to the City of London*, 1649) that it was the poor who would be "picked out and honoured" in the work of putting the world to rights, he was drawing on a tradition which stretched from John Ball to the events which climaxed in the establishment of an English republic. That by 1648 he was thoroughly well read in the radical tradition of the "Everlasting Gospel" there can be no serious doubt.

III
“The indwelling power of Reason”

From ostensibly addressing his former countrymen in Lancashire, Winstanley turns in his next work, *The Breaking of the Day of God*, to his fellow-sectaries and radicals, addressing them as “the despised sons and daughters of Zion”. “Daughters” would henceforth figure no less strongly than “sons” in his polemics: another outrage against entrenched views on the subservience of women, expressed most vehemently in attempts to prohibit women preaching or playing any leadership role. (William Rabisher’s cookery book published in 1661 credited Winstanley as author of the heresy that animals and women, no less than men, had something of God in them, thus crowning him as the true begetter of both feminism - or at least feminist theology - and vegetarianism). Sons and daughters of “Zion” - drawing here on the mythology of a chosen people - are “the objects of the world’s hatred and reproach”, Winstanley writes, “ and in these uproar risings you are condemned to death under the name of roundheads”.

Breaking clearly reflects the critical political situation at the time of writing, and in this it sets a pattern: virtually all of Winstanley’s pamphleteering arises from immediate developments in the revolution through which he was living, and much of it can only be properly understood by reference to its immediate political context. The king’s secret alliance with the Scots had just been uncovered, and a series of “uproar risings” around the country, culminating in the royalist Kent rebellion in May, had precipitated the “second civil war” between Cromwell’s Independent “roundheads” and the king’s new episcopalian-presbyterian alliance. Independents and radicals knew that their hard-won gains were threatened, that a royalist victory would impose upon them a rigid presbyterian discipline no less totalitarian than that they had rebelled against. “You are the men,” writes Winstanley, “they would chain up by an ecclesiastical power and would give no liberty to practice what God teaches you”. But there is good news. “Your redemption is near, for the Lord is burning up the dross of our flesh and shaking down the corruption in kingdoms and churches.” The time is coming when “you shall see these divisions swallowed up in love, so that magistrates shall love the people and the people shall cheerfully obey magistrates”.

Winstanley again based his somewhat startlingly optimistic view that the powerful and the powerless would soon be joined in a common fellowship on his reading of Biblical prophecies. Millenarian speculation was rife in his day, in the mainstream churches no less than among the sectaries. Joachim's third "age of the Spirit" had failed to arrive on time in 1260, but that simply meant that he had failed to read God's timetable correctly. Winstanley offers his own reading of *Revelation* 11:3, in which an angel of God declares that he will give power to two witnesses who will prophesy for 1260 days. The two witnesses, he says, are "Christ in the flesh" - the historical Jesus - and "Christ in the spirit", a Christ-principle dispersed in humankind, "including both learned and unlearned, rich and poor". The 1260 days typify the long period in which "the church shall be in captivity to the anti-Christian power". But this age "is now nearly finished, and the day of Christ begins to shine". "Already the kingdom of Christ begins to appear, among the Saints that are scattered abroad." (By "saints", of course, he meant those who had left the Church for their own gathered congregations: those, we might say, who had taken leave of God for God's sake). "But by the angels of darkness in men they are branded as sectaries, schismatics, Anabaptists, and roundheads." "It is the misery of this age that men try to uphold a usurped ecclesiastical power", fancying that "present troubles would disappear... if all men could be forced to practice one outward, lazy, formal, customary, and tithe-oppressing way of pretended divine worship". Such "ecclesiastical power is not ordained of God but is got by crafty men from kings", setting up "the teaching of men against the teaching of the spirit" and "teaching according to books and authorities against the teaching of the indwelling God". "Men will not believe that God will now give his spirit to tradesmen, as formerly He gave it to fishermen, but believe that only those who have human ordination may teach." However, "the time for this has gone by... Already the sun of righteousness has risen in some, and the bright shining of it will be England's liberty".

Winstanley's third work, *The Saints Paradice*, followed hard on the heels of *The Breaking of the Day*, with the second civil war at its height. "When the counties rose against the Parliament's army some were not ashamed to say that they would destroy men, women, and children of the Independent party. God can make an outside professing service-book man [an episcopalian] kill an outside professing Presbyterian, or he can permit the latter to kill a hypocritical Independent". The "sincere-hearted" simply look on "and are preserved". Winstanley repeats with growing insistence that the coming saints' paradise is to be built not on clerical book-learning and authority but on experience, "experimental knowledge of Christ", "a teacher within". "What I hear another man speak is nothing to me until I find the same experience in myself; the testimony of others is known to be true by the testimony of the same experience within myself." To the horror of a religious establishment which professed to found its authority on the Bible as the word of God, Winstanley, like the Quakers three or four years later, included the scriptures as human writings to be tested by personal experience. "Not the Apostles' writings but the spirit that dwelt in them and inspired their hearts gives life and peace." The same inspiration which gave rise to the apostles' writings was available to all, to be understood as an "inward teacher", tested experimentally. Most ominously for those who distrusted the lower orders as the mob, the poor and ignorant can become "abundantly learned in the experimental knowledge of Christ".

But *The Saints Paradice* also marks a further development in Winstanley's thinking. He is seen moving towards an increasingly mythological and metaphorical interpretation of scripture. In *The Mysterie of God*, the devil was demythologised as selfishness. This is not an external devil but a devil within. "What you call the devil is within you, and you will see that, by the power of the annointing, you will be set free from the devil in a short time". But just as the devil is not a real person, Heaven is not a real place. "Every Saint is a true Heaven, because God dwells in him and he in God, and the communion of Saints is a true Heaven." Angels too are "the sparks of glory or heavenly principles set in men". The day of judgment is a metaphor, as is the resurrection of the dead. Even the Ten Commandments are rejected as a law to which the spirit is superior. But most radical of all, God and Christ begin to be understood in the same way. It is the devil which "leads men to imagine God in a place of glory beyond the skies". God is neither an external being nor a deified historical Jesus. Christ is "not a single man at a distance from you but the indwelling power of reason".

"You are not to be saved by believing that a man lived and died long ago at Jerusalem, but by the power of the spirit within you treading down all unrighteousness of the flesh. Neither are you to look for God in a place of glory beyond the sun, but within yourself and within every man... He that looks for a God outside himself, and worships a God at a distance, worships he knows not what, but is... deceived by the imagination of his own heart". But "he that looks for a God within himself... is made subject to and hath community with the spirit that made all flesh, that dwells in all flesh and in every creature within the globe". God is not so much transcendent as radically immanent, and immanent not just in an historical Jesus but in all humankind - and, indeed, in all living creatures.

How does Winstanley think of this disembodied God? In *The Saints Paradice*, written hard on the heels of his first two pamphlets, he is already beginning to feel his way towards a distinctive theology which, within a year, will motivate his communist experiment. "The spirit of right understanding has taken up his dwelling in this flesh [humankind], and from hence man is called a reasonable creature, which is a name given to no other creature but man, because the spirit of reason acts in him". The "powers of the heart" must "submit to the light of reason" if there is to be "love between all creatures". But what is this "spirit of reason" which has taken up its dwelling in the human species? "The Spirit or Father is pure reason", says Winstanley, and "when flesh becomes subject to the reason within it, it can never act unrighteously or trespass against others, but it does as it would be done by." "Let Reason rule the man, and he dares not trespass against his fellow-creature, but will do as he would be done unto. For Reason tells him, Is thy neighbour hungry and naked today, do thou feed and clothe him; it may be thy case tomorrow, and then he will be ready to help thee." Reason "knits every creature together into a oneness, making every creature to be an upholder of his fellow".

So the devil is human selfishness and all the evil that selfishness entails. God is pure reason. The indwelling of God (or Christ, or the Spirit) in his saints is the growth of reason, which must overcome selfishness. Our cloth merchant turned cowherd turned agitator is saying something new, which will soon be seen to have revolutionary implications for human action.

Indeed, it may be that some of Winstanley's hostile readers understood the revolutionary implications even before he did. His next pamphlet, *Truth Lifting up its Head against Scandals*, seeks to answer some of the scandalised responses to the ideas set out in *Saints Paradice*. The precise date of *Truth's* publication is unclear. The title page says 1649, but it was clearly written before *The New Law of Righteousness*, which begins with a preface dated January 26 1649. *Truth* itself begins with an address "to the scholars of Oxford and Cambridge, and to all that call themselves ministers of the Gospel in city and country", dated October 16 1648, so we may reasonably conjecture that the greater part of the pamphlet was written between October and December of that year and came off the press at the beginning of January 1649.

The address to scholars and ministers mocks them for their

divisions. "One company of you sayes, this translation is the truth; and then the People must be forced to follow you: loe, here is Christ, saith the Prelats; another company of yours saies, such a translation is the truest; and then the People must be forced to follow them... First, here in the Presbytery; then there in the Independency: and thus you lead the People like horses by the noses: & ride upon them at your pleasure from one forme and custome to another, and so quite from the Spirit."

The churches are warning that "there are a company of men rose up that denies God and Christ, and the Scriptures and the Gospel, and prayer, and all Ordinances". Winstanley knows who they mean. "I my selfe being branded by some of your mouths, as guilty of horrid *blasphemy*, for denying all these, as you say, though you cannot prove it, was drawn forth by the Spirit to write what here followes; which I leave to the spirituall men all the world over to judge." Winstanley's italicised emphasis on the word "blasphemy" is a taunt: the 1648 Blasphemy Act had just been passed to put a stop to the radicals' teachings and, in Winstanley's own neighbourhood, had just claimed one of its first victims.

The immediate occasion of *Truth Lifting up its Head* appears to have been the arrest in Kingston, Surrey, of William Everard of Reading. Everard had been cashiered from the army, and was probably the same William Everard who had been implicated in a Leveller army mutiny at Ware in 1647. A William Everard of Reading was associated with the radical mysticism of the Familist-influenced John Pordage and Jakob Boehme in 1649 and again in 1654, and since Boehme and Pordage used the imagery of an "inner light" which Winstanley (followed by George Fox) was to make much use of, we may reasonably guess that these various Everards were one and the same. Everard evidently began an agitation in Kingston, where a "raging multitude (some that call themselves Ministers, and some common people)" caused the bailiffs to put him in prison "upon these supposed scandals". Winstanley probably met him before his arrest, when he "took a nights lodging" in the town.

That Winstanley himself was implicated in Everard's activities is clear from his description of his pamphlet as "a vindication of the man and my selfe, being slandered as well as he (by some of the Ministers), having been in his company". Everard was soon to join with Winstanley in the first dig at George's Hill, which may even have been his own original idea. But at this stage, at the turn of the year, it seems that what was scandalising the good people of Kingston was the identification by Winstanley, in his writings, and perhaps by Everard, in his street agitation, of God and Reason. *Truth Lifting up its Head* is first and foremost a defence and an elaboration of this astonishingly imaginative idea.

IV
The vision

The beginning of 1649 was a truly apocalyptic time. To add to the thousands killed, maimed, widowed and orphaned by civil war, tens of thousands were starving due to a second successive harvest failure. The killing hunger had spread from the countryside into the city of London itself. The Army had seized power in December, but was faced not only with the suppression of its royalist and presbyterian enemies and the preservation of some form of law and order but with the growing threat of Leveller mutiny within its own ranks. Winstanley signed his preface to his next pamphlet, *The New Law of Righteousnes*, on January 26. Four days later, Charles I was beheaded and England was kingless.

In these momentous times, when it seemed to many that the old familiar dispensations had passed away, to be replaced by God only knew what, Winstanley had a "trance". Many words have been wasted over the nature of this trance. Can we take seriously, it has been asked, a political analysis and programme derived not from study and the rational process but from a magical-mystical experience, a supernatural revelation? Proponents of a primarily-theological Winstanley say yes, theological sceptics say no. But the question rests on two misunderstandings. The first is its failure to recognise that Winstanley himself had ceased to believe in a realist God who really revealed real truths: Winstanley's God was an abstract principle of universal justice and community which he called Reason. If his trance was an act of God, it was by definition an act of Reason.

The second misunderstanding has to do with "trance" and what it meant to contemporaries. Christopher Hill has cleared that one up[1]. He calls in aid the *Oxford English Dictionary* to argue that "trance" was used in the seventeenth century to mean "a state of mental abstraction from external things", with no implication whatever of mystical or supernatural cause. In *The Saints Paradice* Winstanley had already noted that God sometimes speaks inwardly by voice, vision, dream or revelation, taking care to make clear that he wasn't referring to "material" voices. When he has a dialogue with God (as recorded in a later pamphlet, *A Watch-word to the City of London*) he again makes it clear that both sides of the dialogue take place "within my heart". (We are reminded of William Blake's answer to the question of where his divine visions came from: he tapped his own forehead). So many of Winstanley's contemporaries had trances, visions, revelations of this kind that Hobbes wrote in 1651 that for a man to say "God hath spoken to him in a dream is no more than to say he dreamed that God spake to him". Winstanley would have agreed. Indeed, he would have insisted that this was precisely his point - adding, no doubt, that the moment of clarity, of sudden understanding, was no less true and real for being firmly located "within my heart". As we shall see, Winstanley's comrade William Everard also acted in obedience to a "vision". Hill is surely right to suggest that these trances, visions and voices each refer to "a moment of clarification in a process of deep meditation".

Winstanley reports his trance at the start of chapter 8 of *The New Law of Righteousnes*: "I was in a trance not long since", when "I heard these words, *Worke together. Eat bread together*; declare this all abroad. Likewise I heard these words. *Whosoever it is that labours in the earth, for any person or persons, that lifts up themselves as Lords & Rulers over others, and that doth not look upon themselves equal to others in the Creation, The hand of the Lord shall be upon that labourer: I the Lord have spoke it and I will do it;* Declare this all abroad".

The New Law, in fifteen chapters, is Winstanley's longest and most comprehensive work to date. In a preface he dedicates it "To the twelve tribes of Israel that are circumcised in heart, and scattered through all the nations of the earth" - that is, to the radical sects he sees as God's (Reason's) new chosen people. They are the seed of Jacob, long "hated, persecuted and despised" as the servant of the powerful Esaus of this world, whose time has now come. Shifting the biblical analogy, "This new Law of righteousness and peace, which is rising up, is David your King", now "coming again the second time in the personall appearance of sons and daughters; he will be a true Davider [divider] indeed, between flesh and spirit, between bondage and libertie, between oppressours and the oppressed; he is and will be the righteous Judge; he will lead your captivitie captive, and set you down in peace".

The work is not to be done by violence, he insists, pointedly addressing those who believed that the New Age was to be inaugurated by the swords of the New Model Army which had just taken power. Winstanley, like the early Quakers, was not always consistent in his attitude to the New Model, which sometimes seemed the indispensable bulwark of the revolution and sometimes the vanguard of reaction. Here, Winstanley does not condemn it for taking power but insists that the continuing reformation is not to be accomplished by military force. "The swords and counsels of flesh shall not be seen in this work, the arm of the Lord onely shall bring these mighty things to passe", as men and women experience "the light of the Father" in their souls, the "dreams, voices and revelations immediately from the Father himself, his own inward teaching". Reason will prevail, as its children rise "like the noise of mighty waters, carrying all before them".

The long-captive "children of Israel" will come into their own, into a state where "all bondage, curse and tears shall be done away": a state, says Winstanley, of which he himself had already "received a taste". But the great liberation, the "saints' paradise", is now given a specific social and economic form. "So long as such are Rulers as cals the Land theirs, upholding this particular propriety [property] of *Mine and Thine*, the common-people shall never have their liberty, nor the Land ever freed from troubles, oppressions and complainings". The Bible's condemnation of wealth and power is constantly evoked, as in the injunction to rich men to "howl and weep, for their gold and silver is cankered, and the rust thereof cries unto heaven for vengeance against them". "Surely," says Winstanley, "all those threatnings shall be materially fullfilled, for they shall be turned out of all, and their riches given to a people that wil bring forth better fruit, and such as they have oppressed shall inherit the Land... Reason requires that every man should live upon the increase of the earth comfortably; though covetousnesse fights against Reasons law". The "beasts of the field" enjoy the land in common: "though they break over hedges, and eat in any pasture, they do not imprison and hang one another, the earth is a common livelyhood for them". So "surely the Father will give as large a liberty to his children to inherit the earth, as he gives to the beast of the field".

Winstanley is at pains to stress that he is not inciting to violence. "I do not speak that any particular man shall go and take their neighbours goods by violence, or robbery (I abhor it)". Such methods, he says acidly, belong only to "setled governments". Instead, Reason, "the Lord Christ", will "spread himself in multiplicities of bodies, making them all of one heart and mind, acting in the righteousness one to another. It must be one power in all, making all to give their consent to confirm the law of righteousness and reason". The new law "shall be so plainly writ in every ones heart, that none shall desire to have more than another, or to be Lord over other, or to lay claim to any thing as his; this phrase of *Mine and Thine* shall be swallowed up in the law of righteous actions one to another, for they shall all live as brethren, every one doing as they would be done by... There shall be no need of Lawyers, prisons, or engines of punishment one over another, for all shall walk and act righteously in the Creation, and there shall be no beggar, nor cause of complaining in all this holy Mountain". It is the vision of *Isaiah, Ezekiel* and *Hosea,* elaborated with reference to the epistle to the *Hebrews,* those of *James* and *I John*, and the *Acts of the Apostles* with its description of the early church as a society whose members had "all things in common".

Landlords would not be forcibly evicted. "If the rich wil stil hold fast this propriety of *Mine and thine*, let them labour their own Land with their own hands", leaving "the Commons, Mountain, and Hils" to "the common-People... that say the earth is ours, not mine." The point was, of course, that as tenants left their landlords to till the commons, the landlord would be forced to reduce his holding to a size he could manage without hired labour. This might induce him, in due course, to see Reason and throw in his lot with the people. And if he did not? "What if some steal or whore, or become idle, and wil not work, but live upon others labours, as rich men do, that cal the land theirs?" They "shal not be imprisoned, hanged or killed... But the punishment of such shal be this, he shal be set to work, and have land appointed him to work upon, and none shal help him... til such time as the spirit in him, make him know himself to be equal to others in the Creation".

In one of the finest and most powerful passages in the noble and poetic vision which is *The New Law of Righteousnes*, Winstanley writes:

"Did the light of Reason make the earth for some men to ingrosse up into bags and barns, that others might be opprest with poverty? Did the light of Reason make this law, that if one man hath not such abundance of the earth as to give to others he borrowed of; that he that did lend should imprison the other, and starve his body in a close room? Did the light of Reason make this law, that some part of man kinde should kil and hang another part of man-kinde, that could not walk in their steps?

"Surely Reason was not the God that made that law; for this is to make one part of the Creation alwaies to be quarrelling against another part; which is mighty dishonour to our Maker. But covetousnesse, that murdering God of the world, was that Law-maker, And that is the God, or ruling power, which all men that claim a particular interest in the earth, do worship."

In a few short crowded months, impelled by the speed of revolutionary change all around him, Winstanley had moved from a theological radicalism which insisted that the poor had a proper place in the scheme of things to the deeply subversive political proposition that the poor must become the agents of their own salvation: must take matters into their own hands and begin to turn the world upside down. In *The New Law of Righteousnes*, Winstanley declared himself a communist.

V
Action: "the life of all"

Winstanley now moved from the propaganda of the word to that of the deed. The moment of truth, of inspiration, which he called a "trance" was a call to action. Nor was he the only one to see clearly what had to be done. As William Everard was reported[1] as telling Lord Fairfax when he and Winstanley appeared before the Lord General on April 20, he too had had a vision "which bad him, Arise, and dig and plow the Earth, and receive the fruits thereof". Part of the common heathland at "George's Hill", between Cobham and Kingston and in the manor of Walton on Thames, was chosen for the first plantation, perhaps because its extent was such that a part of it could be dug without unduly inconveniencing local residents or encroaching on common rights, perhaps because there seemed to be promising indications of local support. It is not clear exactly how many men joined Winstanley and Everard on the first day - one report to the Government suggests there were only four altogether - but fifteen men are named in *The True Levellers Standard Advanced* (with an "etc" added to the last name to indicate that there were more), published in April, and 45 (including Winstanley but not Everard) in *A Declaration from the Poor Oppressed People of England* published in June. The occupation began on April 1 1649 with a breaking of the ground to plant beans, carrots and parsnips, and later barley.

The "True Levellers", as they were soon to style themselves, immediately met opposition. They were attacked by local gangs who tore down their huts and dug up their seeds. They were threatened by soldiers. The pro-Government newsbook *The Kingdomes Faithfull and Impartiall Scout* reported on April 14 of the "new-fangled people that begin to dig on St. Georges Hill" that "The new Plantation in Surrey is re-levelled by the Country people, and many of the Levelling Seekers forced to fly (in the heat of their zeal) for refuge". Other reports in the same paper in the next nine days noted that the diggers "professe they will not fight, knowing that not to be good for them", though one of them, "getting up a great burden of thorns and bryers," had "thrust them into the pulpit at the Church at Walton, to stop out the Parson". On the other hand, when a "Gentleman... strook one of them a box on the eare... the Leveller said it was again[st] their principles to returne it againe, but rather to turn the other eare so the business was soon pacified" [2].

The Diggers - they quickly established themselves as a distinctive group, justifying the capital D - immediately replanted, and on April 16 Henry Sanders of Walton wrote to the Council of State - the military Government - informing them of "a disorderly and tumultuous sort of people asembling themselves together... at a place called St George's Hill". While the Diggers' cause "may seem very ridiculous," he warned, "things of a greater and more dangerous consequence may grow, to the disturbance of the peace and quiet of the commonwealth". The Council had already received intelligence to the effect that "on Sunday sennight last there was one Everard, once one of the army but was cashiered, who termeth himself a prophet, one Stewer [Star] and Coulton and two more, all living in Cobham, came to St George's Hill in Surrey and began to dig on that side of the hill next to Camp Close, and sowed the ground with parsnips, carrots and beans. On Monday following they were there again, being increased in their number, and on the next day, being Tuesday, they fired the heath and burned at least 40 rood of heath, which is a very great prejudice to the Towne".

By the Friday, according to this report, they had grown to twenty or thirty, and on Saturday they had bought barley seed-corn in Kingston market, where they had issued a general invitation to the people to join them. "They do threaten to pull down and level all park pales, and lay open, and intend to plant there very shortly. They give out they will be four or five thousand within ten days, and threaten the neighbouring people there; that they will make them all come to the hills and work; and forewarn them suffering their cattle to come near the plantation; if they do, they will cut their legs off. It is feared they have some design in hand". Finally, it was suggested that the Diggers might be linked with a group of soldiers and others who were said to have invaded Walton church and announced that the Sabbath, tithes, ministers, magistrates and the Bible were all abolished. This may be a garbled account of the event when the Diggers filled the parson's pulpit with thorns and briars to prevent him preaching. Perhaps, as the Quakers would habitually do two or three years later, they took on the minister at his own game and did some preaching themselves.

The Council instructed the Surrey Justices of the Peace to proceed against the ringleaders, and also ordered Colonel Fairfax to despatch troops to disperse the colony and "prevent the like for the future, that a disaffected party may not, under colour of such ridiculous people, rendezvous themselves in order to greater mischief". Fairfax accordingly sent two troops of horse under the command of Captain John Gladman, who reported on April 19 that "the business is not worth the writing nor yet taking notice of: I wonder the Council of State should be so abused with informations". Possibly at their own suggestion, since Gladman considered the business so trivial, it was arranged that Winstanley and Everard would come to London the following day to explain their action to Fairfax himself.

The official newsbook *A Perfect Diurnall of Some Passages in Parliament* reported the meeting: something of a publicity coup for the Diggers. The account puts the Diggers' case in Everard's mouth, but every sentence carries Winstanley's mark. In any case, it is unlikely that he remained silent. Everard is quoted as telling the Lord General that "their intent is to restore the Creation to its former condition. And that as God had promised to make the barren Ground fruitfull: So now, what they did was to renew the ancient Community of the enjoying of fruits of the Earth and to distribute the benefit thereof to the Poore and needy, and to feed the Hungry, and to cloathe the Naked. And that they intend not to meddle with any man's Propriety, nor to break down any Payls or inclosures, but onely to meddle with what was common and untilled, and to make it fruitfull for the use of man; but that the time will suddenly be that all men should willingly come in, and give up their Lands and Estates, and willingly submit to this Community. And for those that will come in and worke, they shall have meat, drinke and clothes, which is all that is necessary for the life of man; and that for money, there was not any need of it, nor of any clothes more then to cover their nakednesse. And that they will not defend themselves by Armes, but will submit unto Authority, and wait till the promised opportunity be offered which they conceive to be neer at hand. And that as their forefathers lived in Tents, so it would be suitable to their condition now to live in the same. With many other things to this purpose."

It seems a fair report for so hostile a source. But the paper did go on to observe that "while Everard and Winstanly were before the Generall they stood with their Hats on, and being demanded the reason, sayd, he was but their fellow Creature". This levelling refusal of "hat honour" to one's supposed social superiors had a pedigree: John Lilburne had refused to doff his hat when tried by the Star Chamber in 1637, and the same symbolic assertion of social equality was to become a badge of the Quakers, who continued with it, despite the outrage and persecution it evoked, through the Republic and on into the Restoration. Fairfax, however, who was used to dealing with unbendingly principled radicals under his own military command, appears not to have taken offence, since he responded to their appeal for military protection with assurances that they would not be disturbed by his soldiers, though he ordered them to cease their activities or face eviction at the hands of the local Justices.

In the midst of their revolutionary act, while doing their best to placate and fend off the hostile mob, defend their temporary homes, and plant and replant their seeds, Winstanley and his comrades found time within these critical early April days to write and prepare for the press another pamphlet, *The True Levellers Standard Advanced*. The main text is clearly mostly if not entirely Winstanley's work, but a preface is signed by John Taylor, one of the 15 co-signatories to the pamphlet itself. The preface is dated April 20 - the very day Winstanley and Everard appeared before Fairfax - and copies were evidently in the booksellers and on the streets within a week, since the copy in the Thomason collection at the British Museum is dated April 26.

True Levellers Standard marks a striking shift of emphasis and style from Winstanley's previous writings. First, and not surprisingly in the circumstances, it is much shorter than *Truth Lifting up its Head* and the fifteen-chapter *New Law*. Secondly, it accelerates the swing, begun in *New Law*, from a theological and biblical emphasis to immediate practical and political considerations. Thirdly, as the title itself demonstrates, there is a new alignment with the Levellers' cause, or at least the cause of a Leveller faction. The shift of emphasis from eschatological theology to present politics is obviously dictated by what was happening there and then, on the ground. The shift towards a secular Leveller rhetoric is more intriguing.

It may be that when their opponents labelled the Diggers Levellers (as we have seen in the newsbooks), Winstanley's comrades defiantly appropriated the term of abuse, much as Ranters were doing and Quakers were to do with their own originally derisive nicknames. But there would seem to be more to it than that. In December 1648 a group of radical Levellers in Buckinghamshire - less than forty miles from Cobham, as Hill points out - had published *Light Shining in Buckinghamshire*, which clearly drew on Winstanley's theology of Reason and co-operation. *Light Shining* also went further than the Leveller leadership (Lilburne, Walwyn and Overton) had ever gone, or ever would go, in hinting that something akin to communism - freedom to enjoy the land "without property one more than another" - was part of their programme. But if the anonymous authors of *Light Shining* drew on Winstanley's 1648 writings, it seems highly likely that Winstanley read their pamphlet and was in turn influenced by it. At a time when the Leveller party itself was in considerable disarray, persecuted by the Army command and even accused of conspiring with royalist elements to bring down the republic that had so disappointed them, it must have seemed good sense to Winstanley and his band to make a bid for a new kind of "True Levelling".

The most obvious borrowing of Leveller doctrine in *The True Levellers Standard Advanced* is the "Norman yoke" myth. Lilburne's Levellers had made good use of this potent piece of radical-underground mythology, which looked back to a pre-Conquest and prelapsarian England of Anglo-Saxon communities living much as John Ball's Adam and Eve had lived, delving and spinning for themselves without the aid of any gentleman class. According to the theory of the Norman yoke, this English paradise was conquered by a foreign people led by William of Normandy who imposed a feudal system, dividing the land between themselves and enslaving freeborn Englishmen. This system had stood for nearly six centuries. Landlords and gentry, magistrates and clergy, lawyers and engrossers were all agents of the "kingly power", the Norman interest. The common people were the true English, struggling to regain their freeborn status by throwing off the Norman yoke. This powerful mix of history and story, nationalism and popular idealism, was probably the single most effective weapon in the Leveller party's propaganda armoury. In taking on the mantle of True Levellers, Winstanley and his comrades made free with their inheritance.

In a preface clearly aimed at countering reports that the Diggers were thieves, malcontents or madmen, John Taylor announces that "I have had some Conversation with the Authour of this ensuing Declaration, and the Persons Subscribing, and by experience find them sweetly acted and guided by the everlasting spirit, the Prince of Peace, to walk in the paths of Righteousness, not daring to venture upon any acts of injustice; but endeavouring to do unto all, as they would have done to them, having Peace and Joy in themselves, knit together and united in one Spirit of Glory and Truth, Love to their fellow Creatures, Contentation with Food and Rayment, shewing much Humility and Meekness of spirit". This is contrasted with the condition of their oppressors, slaves to "the God of this world", those who are "making Lawes under specious pretences, yea and penalties too". "I know you have high thoughts of your selves," Taylor continues, "think you know much, and see much, but the Light that is in you is Darknesse". But they are not without the possibility of redemption. "Oh that Reason might sit upon the throne of your hearts and Iudge... If you could speak impartially, your own Consciences can bear me witnesse."

Winstanley's own text is headed "A Declaration to all the Powers of England, and to all the Powers of the World, shewing the cause why the common people of England have begun, and gives consent to digge up, manure, and sowe corn upon George-Hill in Surrey; by those that have subscribed, and thousands more that gives consent". It begins with the familiar invocation of a Paradise lost:

"In the beginning of Time, the great Creator Reason, made the Earth to be a Common Treasury, to preserve Beasts, Birds, Fishes, and Man, the lord that was to govern this Creation". But selfishness (Winstanley's Devil) had come in, "ruling as King in the room of Reason", whereupon the earth "was hedged in to In-closures by the teachers and rulers, and the others were made Servants and Slaves", so that what was once "a Common Store-house for all, is bought and sold, and kept in the hands of a few". But the time is come when "the Prophecies of Scriptures and Reason" are to be fulfilled and "the Earth becomes a Common Treasury again".

However, there are those who stand in the way of Paradise regained, and Winstanley says exactly who they are. He turns his wrath on Cromwell and the Generals and the whole apparatus of a republic in which so many hopes had been placed, only to be dashed and trampled underfoot.

"O thou Powers of *England*, though thou hast promised to make this People a Free People, yet thou hast so handled the matter, through thy self-seking humour, That thou hast wrapped us up more in bondage, and oppression lies heavier upon us; not only bringing thy fellow Creatures, the Commoners, to a morsel of Bread, but confounding all sorts of people by thy Government, of doing and undoing.

"First, Thou hast made the people to take a Covenant and Oaths to endeavour a Reformation, and to bring in Liberty every man in his place; and yet while a man is in pursuing of that Covenant, he is imprisoned and oppressed by thy Officers, Courts, and Justices, so called.

"Thou hast made Ordinances to cast down Oppressing, Popish, Episcopal, Self-willed and Prerogative Laws; yet we see, That Self-wil and Prerogative power, is the great standing Law, that rules all in action, and others in words.

"Thou hast made many promises and protestations to make the Land a Free Nation: And yet at this very day, the same people, to whom thou hast made such Protestations of Liberty, are oppressed by thy Courts, Sizes,

Sessions, by thy Justices and Clarks of the Peace, so called, Bayliffs, Committees, are imprisoned, and forced to spend that bread, that could save their families from Famine.

"And all this, Because they stand to maintain an universal Liberty and Freedom, which not only is our Birthright, which our Maker gave us, but which thou hast promised to restore unto us, from under the former oppressing Powers that are gone before, and which likewise we have bought with our Money, in Taxes, Free-quarter, and Bloud-shed; all which Sums thou hast received at our hands, and yet thou hast not given us our bargain."

Winstanley sets out six reasons for the digging. First, to "lay the Foundation making the Earth a Common Treasury for All, both Rich and Poor", as moved "by Vision, Voyce and Revelation". The land has been stolen since "the enslaving Conquest... and from that time, Kings, Lords, Judges, Justices, Bayliffs, and the violent bitter people that are Free-holders, are and have been Successively: the *Norman* Bastard *William* himself, his Colonels, Captains, inferiour Officers, and Common Souldiers, who still are from that time to this day in pursuite of that victory, Imprisoning, Robbing, and killing the poor enslaved *English* Israelites.

"And this appears cleer, For when any Trustee or state Officer is to be Chosen, The Free-holders or Landlords must be the Chusers, who are the *Norman* Common Souldiers, spred abroad in the Land; And who must be Chosen? but some very rich man, who is the Successor of the *Norman* Colonels or high Officers. And to what end have they been thus Chosen? but to Establish that *Norman* power the more forcibly over the enslaved *English*, and to beat them down again, when as they gather heart to seek for Liberty...

"O what mighty Delusion, do you, who are the powers of *England*, live in! That while you pretend to throw down that *Norman* yoke, and *Babylonish* power, and have promised to make the groaning people of *England* a Free People; yet you still lift up that *Norman* yoke, and slavish Tyranny, and hold the People as much in bondage, as the Bastard Conqueror himself, and his Councel of War."

And in a thunderous climax to this, the first of his six arguments:

"Take notice, That *England* is not a Free people, till the Poor that have no Land, have a free allowance to dig and labour the Commons, and so live as Comfortably as the Landlords that live in their Inclosures. For the People have not laid out their Monies, and shed their Bloud, that their Landlords, the *Norman* power, should still have its liberty and freedom to rule in Tyranny... but that the Oppressed might be set Free, Prison doors opened, and the Poor peoples hearts comforted by an universal Consent of making the Earth a Common Treasury, that they may live together as one House of Israel, united in brotherly love in one Spirit; and having a comfortable livelihood in the Community of one Earth their Mother."

Secondly, George-Hill was dug because "it was shewed us by Vision in Dreams, and out of Dreams, That that should be the Place we should begin upon". But "not only this Common, or Heath should be taken in and Manured by the People, but all the Commons and waste Ground in *England*, and in the whole World".

Thirdly, the digging fulfilled biblical prophecy. *Ezekiel*, *Jeremiah*, *Isaiah*, *Zacharia*, *Daniel*, *Hosea*, *Joel*, *Amos*, *Obadiah*, *Micah*, *Habakkuk* and *Zephania* are rounded up from the Old Testament, and Paul's epistle to the *Romans* from the New, to demonstrate that "the Spirit of Christ, which is the Spirit of universal Community and Freedom is risen, and is rising, and will rise higher and higher".

Fourthly, the digging was begun in obedience to the visionary command to "*Worke together, Eate Bread together, Declare this all abroad*". The "declaration" was made first by word of mouth, then by writing (the *New Law*), and finally "by Action". Winstanley here takes the opportunity to expand on his "trance": "Another Voice that was heard was this, *Israel shall neither take Hire, nor give Hire*". This outlaws wage labour, a point underlined by the rest of the trance-message: "*Whoever labours the Earth for any Person or Persons, that are lifted up to rule over others, and doth not look upon themselves, as Equal to others in the Creation: The hand of the Lord shall be upon that Labourer: I the Lord have spoke it, and I will do it*". "This", says Winstanley, in a commentary on his Voice's message, "Declares likewise to all Laborors... that they shall not dare work for Hire... for by their labours, thay have lifted up Tyrants and Tyranny; and by denying to labor for Hire, they shall pull them down again. He that works for another, either for Wages, or to pay him Rent, works unrighteously".

Fifthly, the inspiration for the dig is "the streaming out of Love in our hearts towards all; to enemies as well as friends; we would have none live in Beggery, Poverty, or Sorrow". Therefore "we shall not be startled, neither at Prison nor Death, while we are about this work; and we have bin made to sit down and count what it may cost us in undertaking such a work, and we know the full sum, and are resolved to give all that we have to buy this Pearl which we see in the Field".

Lastly, "we have another encouragement that this work shall prosper, Because we see it to be the Fulness of Time". As Christ had come to overthrow the work of hypocritical priests, and Moses before him, "Even so now, Professors [of religion] do rest upon the bare observations of Forms and Customs, and pretend to the Spirit, and yet persecutes, grudges, and hates the power of the Spirit... All places stink with the abomination of Self-seeking Teachers and Rulers: For do not I see that every one Preacheth for money, Counsels for money, and fights for money to maintain particular Interests... The common People are filled with good words from Pulpits and Councel Tables, but no good Deeds; for they wait and wait for good, and for deliverances, but none comes". Here again are the precursors of the most militant and persistent anti-clerical movement in English history: the Quakers.

Barely a year after his first venture into print, Gerrard Winstanley has achieved a new eloquence, born of bitter experience and anger. "Truly you Counsellors and Powers of the Earth," he writes, "know this, That wheresoever there is a People, thus united by Common Community of livelihood into Oneness, it will become the strongest Land in the World, for then they will be as one to defend their Inheritance; and Salvation (which is Liberty and Peace) is the Walls and Bulwarks of that Land or City... And thus you Powers of England, and of the whole World, we have declared our Reasons, why we have begun to dig upon George hill in Surrey".

As the Government itself had decisively cut free from the Levellers, so Winstanley's True Levellers had now abandoned any illusion that the true common-wealth would be advanced by those who had taken power. This was not their final position: Winstanley would later see the army, the republican regime and Cromwell himself as potential allies. But that was not how they saw things in April 1649, after three or four weeks of direct action, civil disobedience and violent persecution.

Strong as Winstanley believed his "people united by common community" to be, and despite Fairfax's half-promise of protection, the George's Hill commune was quickly uprooted yet again. The tone of Winstanley's next pamphlet, his *Declaration from the Poor Oppressed People of England*, published at the end of May (Thomason's copy is dated June 1), is so much more belligerent than anything he had written before that Sabine thought it likely that others beside Winstanley, of the 45 who signed it, had had a hand in the writing. But given the savagery of the attacks he had suffered, and perhaps in view of the Government's new May offensive against the Levellers and other radical critics, the tone is understandable even if it is Winstanley's alone. The sense of betrayal by a Government on which so many of the hopes of the Good Old Cause had rested was intense and widespread. Winstanley would not have been exempt from it.

The May *Declaration* repeats the message of *The True Levellers Standard Advanced*: property, money, wage labour, rents are the fruits of the Devil, selfishness, and the time has come for them to be abolished. Those who defend the old system, those to whom the *Declaration* is addressed, hold their power by the murder and thievery of their ancestors: "and that sin of your Fathers, shall be visited upon the Head of you, and your Children, to the third and fourth Generation, and longer too, till your bloody and theeving power be rooted out of the land".

What is new in the *Declaration* is the announcement that the Diggers will no longer content themselves with planting the commons and wastes but now lay claim, in the name of the "poor oppressed people", to the common woods and forests. They give notice that they intend to cut down not only such trees as they may need for their own use, but wood to sell in order to maintain their righteous experiment. Winstanley notes that Lords of the Manor have been putting it about that, far from helping the poor, the Diggers are spoiling the commons for those who hold common rights of grazing, turbary or wood-gathering: a poor argument, he says, from those who are notorious for overstocking the commons with their own sheep and cattle, enclosing when they can and checking traditional access for cutting wood, heath and turfs. These landlords are solemnly warned to stop cutting down trees on the commons for their own private use and profit, and "wood-mongers" are warned to "disown all such private merchandize, as being a robbing of the poor and oppressed". They might buy wood from the poor, "from such as may be appointed by us to sell it", but from no others. "If you will slight us in this thing, blame us not, if we make stop of the Carts you send and convert the Woods to our own use, as need requires, it being our own, equal with him that calls himself the Lord of the Mannor, and not his peculiar right." That such action was contrary to the laws of the land - "Norman" laws - meant nothing. It was their resolve "to observe the Law of righteous action, endeavouring to shut out of the Creation the cursed thing, called *Particular Propriety*, which is the cause of all wars, bloud-shed, theft, and enslaving Laws, that hold the people under miserie".

It is noticeable that only eight of the 15 signatories to *True Levellers* were still around to sign the *Declaration*. William Everard and John Taylor are among the missing names. But the *Declaration* boasted 37 new signatories. The colony was growing, if not at the rate Everard had boasted of in Kingston when he predicted that they would quickly be thousands-strong. Christ might yet rise in sons and daughters, in his own time and at his own pace.

VI
Levellers Old and New

That Winstanley found time to write at all during those climactic days of April and May is astonishing. Within days of the start of the dig, the whole community had been rounded up by locals and marched off to Walton church, where they were shut in till a magistrate ordered their release. Returning to George's Hill, they found their seeds uprooted and their huts dismantled. No sooner had they replanted and rebuilt when a crowd said to be a hundred strong rounded them up and hauled them off to Kingston in an attempt to bring them before the manor court. However, all this meant that the happenings on George's Hill were the talk of that new constituency in English life, the readers of a national press. The London papers were full of it. To some, the Diggers were figures of fun: "a company of crack brains, which are digging out their own ruines". To others, it was a dangerous business when tradesmen and cowherds "begin to perk up in a little knowledge of the scriptures" to "have the world believe they have dreamt Dreams, seen Visions, heard strange voices, and have dictates beyond mans teaching". One paper warned "...what this fanaticall insurrection may grow into cannot be conceived; for Mahomet had as small, and as despicable a beginning, whose damnable infections have spread themselves many hundred years since, over the face of halfe the Universe"[1]. Winstanley could fairly boast that "our digging upon that Common is the talk of the whole land" [2].

One result of the action itself and the publicity it attracted was to sharpen debate in the wider Leveller movement, itself now under relentless attack from the military Government. The Levellers had always been sensitive to the charge that the reforms they proposed, particularly the extension of the franchise to include unpropertied males, would threaten property itself and open the door to communism. Commissary-General Henry Ireton, in the Putney debates of November 1647, had insisted that the Levellers' demands "would go that way to take away all property", and the issue had continued to plague the movement. In December 1648 they had amended their proposed Agreement of the People (the so-called second Agreement entitled *Foundations of Freedom*) to exclude wage-earners and servants, though a further revision in May 1649 omitted the exclusion of wage-earners. The same revision, however, published at the very time the

London press was running hard with the George's Hill shock-horror communist "insurrection" story, included an undertaking that the Levellers' proposed new representative parliament would be expressly forbidden to "levell mens Estates, destroy Propriety, or make all things common". The Leveller leaders themselves were at pains to distance themselves from any appearance of sympathy towards "economic levelling". William Walwyn insisted that the abolition of private property could only come about by "an universall assent thereunto from all and every one of the People", which, on the face of it, was not far removed from Winstanley's faith that "Christ rising" would indeed bring about universal assent, except that Walwyn clearly considered such an outcome extremely remote. "The Community amongst the primitive Christians", he reminded the religious radicals, "was Voluntary, not Coactive."

John Lilburne was far more hostile, claiming in words that nineteenth-century Manchester Liberals and twentieth-century Thatcherites would have been happy to use themselves that the Levellers were "the truest and constantest assertors of liberty and propriety, which are quite opposite to community and levelling", and that there was nothing in their writings or declarations "that doth in the least tend to the destruction of liberty and propriety or to the setting up of levelling by universal community or anything really and truly like it". Indeed, "this conceit of levelling of property and magistracy is so ridiculous and foolish an opinion, as no man of brains, reason or ingenuity, can be imagined such a sot as to maintain such a principle", not least because it would "destroy all industry" by rewarding "every lazy, simple, dronish sot... yea every coward and base low-spirited fellow", no less than the "valiant" hard-worker. Fear of "spongers" is no modern Tory invention, but we do not expect to see it expressed quite so virulently in the mouth of "Freeborn John".

Clearly not all Leveller activists were happy with their leaders' attempts to accommodate the party's radicalism to the realities of Army power, and particularly with the express identification of the party with the economic interests of the "middling sort" rather than the poor, and the urban rather than the rural underprivileged. The anonymous *Light Shining in Buckinghamshire* of December 1648 and *More Light Shining in Buckinghamshire* of March 1649, while they contain no explicit attack on property, are nevertheless more uncompromisingly radical in tone than the national leadership's pronouncements, and the same group's *A Declaration from the Wel-affected of the County of Buckinghamshire* of May 10 1649, after denouncing the post-royal regimes of Parliament and Army for being "as Arbitrary as those that were before them", goes on to resolve to "further and help the said poor to manure, dig, &c. the said Commons, and to fell those woods growing thereon to help them to a stock, &c.", adding that "All wel-affected persons that joyn in community in Gods way, as those [in] *Acts* 2, and desire to manure, dig, and plant in the waste grounds and Commons, shall not be troubled or molested by any of us, but rather furthered therein".

Sabine[3] notes that, according to the news-sheet *The Kingdom's Faithfull Scout*, these resolutions to support and extend the activities on George's Hill had been adopted at a meeting of Levellers in Aylesbury at the beginning of May, suggesting "the hypothesis that there was a group of extreme Levellers here", just across the river from Surrey. The Diggers' actions, therefore, and particularly their provocative adoption of the name "True Levellers", must be seen as part of the crisis in the Leveller movement as it veered between caution, with the aim of retaining what little influence it still had with the Army high command, and a renewed radicalism born of growing disillusionment and despair at the inability of the national leadership to give the poor and propertyless a stake in the new-born republic.

Certainly the Army Council had more pressing troubles to deal with than the "True Levellers" of George's Hill. Leveller units in the army itself had been agitating for weeks for improved representation and better pay and conditions. On May 1 the rebellion became serious as some regiments refused to be sent to Ireland and began plotting insurrection against their officers. The mutiny was put down at Burford, and the public execution of three agitators selected at random effectively ended Leveller power in the army. Official Levelling, a levelling by politics and state power, seemed a dead end. True Levelling, by direct action rather than word, and by non-violence rather than the sword, seemed to some a new and more promising beginning.

On May 26, on his way back to London after crushing the Burford Levellers, Fairfax made an unexpected visit to the True Levellers at George's Hill. Twelve men were at work and, despite the repeated trampling of crops by their opponents, some barley was beginning to sprout. Fairfax took no action, to the fury of the local freeholders. A day or two later, a group of foot soldiers under a Captain Stravie who were quartered nearby, took matters into their own hands. Only one man and a boy were working the land when they marched on the colony, and, as Winstanley complained to Fairfax, "before any word of provocation was spoken to them, [they] fell upon those two, beating the boy, and took away his coat off his back, and some linnen and victualls that they had, beating and wounding the man very dangerously, and fired our house".

Winstanley made his complaint in an open *Letter to the Lord Fairfax*, delivered on June 9 (two days after a National Day of Thanksgiving for God's deliverance of England from levelling) and printed a few days later. Despite the assaults, by troops under Fairfax's command, the tone is notably restrained. While the colonists were disappointed to receive destruction from the military rather than the protection Fairfax had seemed to promise, the General was told that "for your own particular, we are assured of your moderation and friendship to us, who have ever been your friends in times of straits". Where the whole of the new republican regime, only a few days earlier, had been castigated in the *Declaration from the Poor Oppressed People* as successors of the Norman bastard, maintaining the Norman yoke with no less determination than that of the royalist system they had overturned, Fairfax himself, architect of Burford, was now addressed as one of "our brethren (as an English Tribe)", one who "endeavour[ed] to advance the same King of righteousnesse with us". The old Roundhead General had promised that they would not be treated as enemies until they proved themselves such by their actions. Winstanley evidently took the view that his best hope was to keep, if not the positive goodwill, at least the passive neutrality of the Army, and we might read this as a modification of his denunciations of the previous month. It is certainly a striking testament to his diplomacy that, after these early skirmishes with local troops, the Army did not intervene for many more months. That the True Levellers could deal so cordially with the man who had just killed off the Levellers' cause where it most threatened the inheritors of the Norman yoke is also potent evidence of the gulf that had opened up between moderates and radicals on the revolutionary left.

Winstanley's letter was, of course, not just a private communication. It was intended from the start for publication as part of the propaganda war which was raging as the digging became "the talk of the whole Land; some approving, some disowning". Winstanley cast the war as "a pitched battaile between the Lamb and the Dragon, between the Spirit of love, humility and righteousnesse, which is the Lamb appearing in flesh; and the power of envy, pride, and unrighteousnesse, which is the Dragon appearing in the flesh". The concept of the "Lamb's war", derived from *Revelation*, would be at the heart of Quakerism two or three years later.

Again the Norman yoke analogy was evoked, and also the "younger brother" myth: the notion that the common people of England were the new Israelites, spiritual descendants of Israel, formerly named Jacob, younger brother of Esau, thief of birthrights and thereby a type of all rulers. The Biblical imagery and references would of course have been utterly familiar to the old Puritan general.

Winstanley manages a note of remarkable optimism at the start of his letter. "When you were at our Works upon the Hill," he reminds Fairfax, "we told you, many of the Country-people that were offended at first, begin now to be moderate, and to see righteousnesse in our work, and to own it, excepting one or two covetous Free-holders, that would have all the Commons to themselves, and that would uphold the Norman Tyranny over us, which by the victorie that you have got over the Norman Successor, is plucked up by the roots, therefore ought to be cast away. And we expect, that these our angry neighbours, whom we never wronged, nor will not wrong, will in time see their furious rashnesse to be their folly, and become moderate, to speak and carry themselves like men rationally, and leave off pushing with their hornes like beasts." It was a somewhat forlorn hope.

The letter goes on to disabuse Fairfax - and the wider readership - of popular misconceptions about the Diggers and their relations with the world. They are "not against any that would have Magistrates and Laws to govern, as the Nations of the world are governed", though they would need neither magistrates nor laws themselves when all was held in common. Again, if some wish to "call the Inclosures [their] own land... we are not against it". They would not interfere with private land if private landlords did not interfere with their use of the commons. "No, no, we freely declare, that our corn and cattell, or what we have, shall be freely laid open, for the safety and preservation of the Nation, and we as younger brothers, living in love with you our elder brothers... shall endeavour to do, as we would be done unto; that is, to let every one injoy the benefit of the Creation, to have food and rayment free by the labour of his hands from the earth."

Another misconception was the charge heard from the pulpits that the Diggers proposed to force their heretical religious teachings on their neighbours and destroy the national church. "As for spirituall teachings," Winstanley answers, "we leave every man to stand and fall to his own Master: if the power of covetousnesse be his Master or King that rules in his heart, let him stand and fall to him; let the bodies of men act love, humility, and righteousnesse one towards another, and let the Spirit of righteousnesse be the Teacher, Ruler and Judge both in us and over us; and by thus doing, we shall honor our Father, the Spirit that gave us our being. And we shall honor our Mother the earth, by labouring her in righteousnesse, and leaving her free from oppression and bondage." Yet again there is a pre-echo of Quakerism in both the principle of toleration and the reliance placed not on authority and scripture but on the direct inspiration of a "Teacher... both in us and over us". The pre-echo grows in the next paragraph (with its fascinating premonition of more modern "left brain/right brain" distinctions):

"We shall then honor the higher powers of the left hand man, which is our hearing, seeing, tasting, smelling, feeling, and walk in the light of reason and righteousnesse... and we shall be strengthened by those five well springs of life, of the right hand man, which is, understanding, will, affections, joy and peace, and so live like men, in the light and power of the Son of righteousnesse within our selves feelingly. What need then have we of any outward, selfish, confused Laws made, to uphold the power of covetousnesse, whenas we have the righteous Law written in our hearts."

Having, as he saw it, set the record straight on these matters, Winstanley goes on to ask Fairfax and the Council to put a number of pointed rhetorical questions to "your Lawyers". Was not William the Conqueror king solely by conquest? Was not Charles I his successor as slave-master? Did not the lords of manors hold their title from the Conqueror and his successors? Had they not lost their title, now that "the common People of England, as well as some of the Gentry [quite a concession, that!] have conquered King Charles"? Had not William dispossessed not only the men represented in Parliament but the whole body of the English people? Should not the whole body, then, rather than just the gentry, be given back their freedom? If not, "It had been better for the common people there had been no such conquest [over Charles]; for they are impoverished in their estates by Free-quarter and Taxes, and made worse to live then they were before. But seeing they have paid Taxes, and given Free-quarter according to their estates, as much as the Gentry to theirs, it is both reason and equity that they should have the freedom of the land for their livelihood, which is the benefit of the commons, as the Gentry hath the benefit of their inclosures". Should not the royalists' laws be "cut off with the Kings head?"

While the lawyers puzzle out these questions, the "publike Preachers" should be asked "whether the earth with her fruits, was made to be bought and sold from one to another? and whether one part of mankind was made a Lord of the land, and another part a servant, by the law of Creation before the fall?" The question was "not to be answered by any text of Scripture... but the answer is to be given in the light of it self, which is the law of righteousnesse, or that Word of God that was in the beginning, which dwells in mans heart".

Did not the clergy's own scripture - "your Scripture" - teach that wars and bloodshed were caused by one lording over another? Did it not condemn covetousness? If their God was no respecter of persons, why should they be? Should not the preachers "talk lesse, and live more actually in the power of universall righteousnesse"? Did the King of righteousness bid them love or hate their enemies? "If you say love them, then I demand of you, why do some of you in your Pulpits, and elsewhere, stir up the people to beat, to imprison, put to death or banish, or not to buy and sell with those that endeavour to restore the earth to a common treasury again? Surely at the worst, you can make them but your enemies; therefore love them, win them by love, do not hate them, they do not hate you."

Finally, was it not a breach of the National Covenant to give freedom to clergy and gentry and deny it to the rest? By what right did the gentry still claim rent and the clergy tithes - "a practise which Christ, the Apostles and Prophets never walked in"? It was the clergy, not the True Levellers, who were "false Christs and false Prophets that are risen up in these latter daies".

The letter is a magnificent polemic, Winstanley at the height of his powers. He knows how to play on Fairfax's moderation and past sympathies with the common people who had manned his New Model Army, and he knows too that if he is to win public sympathy for the Diggers' cause he must position that cause as one part of the historic struggle for freedom which the Army itself had proclaimed as its own Good Old Cause.

According to a postscript added to the published version of the *Letter*, it was "delivered by the Authours own hand to the Generall, and the chief Officers, and they very mildly promised they would read it, and consider of it". For the next few weeks the army kept away from George's Hill. The same could not be said of the colonists' civil enemies.

VII
The Lamb's war

On June 11, only two days after Winstanley delivered his letter to Fairfax, and while the text was still at the printers, four Diggers were preparing the ground for the winter season when a large crowd, apparently all women, approached the colony led by two local freeholders on horseback, William Starr and John Taylor. On arrival, the women threw off their coats to reveal themselves as men, carrying staffs and clubs. According to Winstanley's account, the Diggers tried to reason with them, saying they would willingly attend court if charges were laid against them. But "those furious divells Taylor and Starr" had not come to discuss points of law. Without a word, "but like bruit beasts that have no understanding, they fell furiously" on their victims, "beating and striking those foure naked [unarmed] men, beating them to the ground, breaking their heads, and sore bruising their bodies, whereof one is so sore bruised, that it is feared he will not escape with his life".

All four were left for dead, and it was some time before three of them recovered sufficiently to get back to the rest of the colony, bringing the worst-wounded in a cart. Winstanley immediately set to work to publicise the attack in a new pamphlet, *A Declaration of the Bloudie and Unchristian Acting of William Star and John Taylor of Walton*. (William Star may have been a kinsman of Thomas Starre or Star, one of the 15 Diggers who had signed *The True Levellers Standard Advanced* and the 45 who had put their names to *A Declaration from the Poor Oppressed People of England*. John Taylor was presumably not the same man who had written the laudatory preface to the earlier of the two pamphlets, unless he had swiftly recanted. His name, however, is missing from the second work and subsequent Digger tracts).

"Surely this fury in the free-holders", Winstanley writes, "declares plainly, that they got their Lands, both they and their Fathers, by murder, violence and theft, and they keep it by the same power in regard they will not speak like men, but fight and devoure like beasts. Well let the world take notice, that we that do justifie this cause of digging, have obeyed the Lord, in setting forward this work of endeavouring to bring the earth into a Community, and we have peace and purposes to go on."

Winstanley then presses home, in powerful and moving prose, his argument that the civil wars of recent years are giving way to the Lamb's war. England has suffered "dashing one power against another, changing times and customes... Every one that seems to prevaile over another, saies, God gave him the victory, though his conquest be tyranny over his brother, making the King of Righteousnesse the Author of sorrowes, and comfort, not knowing the distinction between the power of darknesse and the power of light: Victories that are got by the sword, are but victories of the Murtherer, and the joy of those victories is but the joy of Cain, when he had killed his brother Abel".

The civil wars had not been a contest between the good and the bad, the godly and ungodly, as the victors would have the world believe, but "Dragon against Dragon, Beast against Beast, Covetousnesse and Pride against Covetousnesse and Pride". "The Dragon hath fought against the Dragon, and one part conquered another." But that was to change. "Thou now begin'st to fight against the Lamb, the Dove, the meek Spirit, the power of love... Well, thou hast rejoyced in thy former victories one beast over another, and thou hast had, and may have seeming victories over the Lamb, and may rejoyce; but know, that this stone (which is alone) against whom thou hast begun to lift up thy heel, shall grind thee to powder. Love suffers under thy furie, love suffers under thy hypocrisie, under thy pride, carelesse, covetous, hard-hearted, self-seeking children. Love bears all things patiently, he suffers thee to reproach, to fight, to oppose, and to rejoyce in doing those things. Love secretly seeks thy preservation, but thou openly seekest his destruction, and glories like a man that hath put off his armour at every seeming shew of victory: but the battell between the Dragon and the Lamb is begun in the midst of thee, and a few years now will let all the world see who is strongest, love or hatred, freedom or bondage."

The new rulers of England, the victors over the old royal tyranny, now face a new opponent: the Lord, the Prince of Peace. Reason. "He calls for Peace, thou cal'st for war, he calls to Freedome, thou cal'st still for bondage, he saith put up thy Sword and live in love, thou saist draw the Sword against all that will live in love. Well, England take thy course, but know for all this thou shalt come to Judgement."

The *Declaration of the Bloudie and Unchristian Acting* is one of Winstanley's shortest pamphlets. It is not signed by him, but its style is signature enough. It reads as if it were dashed off in an hour or two, immediately following the June 11 attack. In seven paragraphs it combines anger and compassion, faith and determination. The True Levellers have declared a third civil war, quite different from its immediate predecessors. This will be a war in which the Lamb, the Dove, will renounce the Dragon's sword in favour of love and reason. Winstanley betrays no doubt as to which will be the ultimate winner.

His optimism was evidently derived from religious faith rather than from any perceived prospect of a let-up in the persecution the Diggers were now facing. Until publication of the *Declaration from the Poor Oppressed People of England*, opposition had been violent but spasmodic, the work of local mobs rather than the gentry. But the *Declaration* changed that. So long as the colonists merely dug an acre or two of uncultivatable heath, they could be regarded as undesirable nuisances rather than serious threats to anyone's pocket. But the *Declaration* had warned landlords that their rights of commonage, and in particular their rights to cut and sell wood, would henceforth come under increasing attack. No doubt this threat helped provoke the "bloudie and unchristian" attack of freeholders Starr and Taylor and their gang of armed "women". More seriously still, it led to a direct legal challenge to Winstanley and his followers.

On June 23 a series of suits for trespass were begun against the Diggers in the Court of Record at Kingston, which had jurisdiction over Walton parish, including George's Hill. The suits were brought in the names of three local gentlemen: Sir Ralph Verney, an absentee who was living as an exile in France, having been expelled from the House of Commons in 1645; Thomas, Viscount Wenman, MP for Oxfordshire in the Long Parliament till excluded by Pride's Purge in 1648; and Richard Winwood, a kinsman of Verney. These three were acting with Francis Drake, lord of the manor of Walton on Thames and himself a victim of Pride's Purge. The four were closely connected by family intermarriages, and Sabine[1] suggests that Drake may have brought the suits in the names of Verney, Wenman and Winwood because they were trustees for the manor under a marriage settlement or some such family arrangement. What was clear, however, was that the scene was set for a pitched battle of wits between the landed gentry, with their links of power and sympathy to the republic's old enemies, and the landless who had dared to stake their own claim to the fruits of revolution. Drake *v* Winstanley epitomised the Dragon *v* the Lamb.

Winstanley refused to hire a lawyer, and the court refused to hear him without. After several unsuccessful attempts to persuade the court to let him plead his own cause, and perhaps those of his fellow-Diggers named in the suits, Winstanley entered a written defence. This too was rejected on the ground that it was not framed in appropriate legal language. On July 28 Winstanley was assessed for damages at £10 (the plaintiffs had asked for £20) plus 29s 1d costs. On his refusal to pay, bailiffs seized eleven cows and a bull he was pasturing (an indication that, while running the colony, he was still earning a living as a cowherd), but these had to be released when it was apparent that he was not their owner. Others named in the suits had damages assessed against them of between £4 and £10, with one Digger, Henry Bickerstaffe, being committed to prison for non-payment (though he was released after three days)[2].

Ever watchful for opportunities to wage the propaganda war - for the Lamb and the Dove needed all the help they could get - Winstanley decided to go over the heads of the Kingston Justices and launch two public appeals, one to the House of Commons and the other to the City of London and the Army. His *Appeal to the House of Commons* was printed on July 11 and presented to the House on July 24, four days before the Kingston judgment. His *Watch-word to the City of London and the Armie* carried a prefatory address dated August 26 (signed "Jerrard Winstanly") and was published early the following month. Much of the *Watch-word*, however, consists of the text of Winstanley's plea to the court, and it will be convenient to look at it first.

Winstanley first sets out his credentials as one of the City's "sons by freedome", no doubt a reference to his former membership of the Company of Master Merchant Taylors. He had paid his dues - "I was free to offer my Mite into thy publike Treasury Guild-hall" - till "by thy cheating sons in the theeving art of buying and selling, and by the burdens of, and for the Souldiery in the beginning of the war, I was beaten out both of estate and trade" and forced into "a Countrey-life" dogged by taxes and free-quarter, by which "my weak back found the burthen heavier then I could bear". After years of bitter sufferings, "my heart was filled with sweet thoughts, and many things were revealed to me which I never read in books, nor heard from the mouth of any flesh... and amongst those revelations this was one, *That the earth shall be made a common Treasury of livelihood to whole mankind, without respect of persons*; and I had a voice within me bad me declare it all abroad, which I did obey, for I declared it by word of mouth wheresoever I came, then I was made to write a little book, called *The new Law of righteousnesse*, and therein I declared it..."

And then, in perhaps the best-known and most inspirational of all his texts:

"...yet my mind was not at rest, because nothing was acted, and thoughts run in me, that words and writings were all nothing, and must die, for action is the life of all, and if thou dost not act, thou dost nothing."

So "I tooke my spade and went and broke the ground upon George-hill in Surrey, thereby declaring freedome to the Creation, and that the earth must be set free from intanglements of Lords and Landlords, and that it shall be a common Treasury to all". But "the old Norman Prerogative Lord of that Mannour Mr Drake, caused me to be arrested for a trespasse against him", and the purpose of this pamphlet was to bring to the City's attention "the unrighteous proceedings of Kingstone Court... that you may consider the case that England is in; all men have stood for freedom, thou hast kept fasting daies, and prayed in morning exercises for freedom; thou hast given thanks for victories, because [of] hopes of freedome". Now the common enemy - the royalists - are gone, but "you are all like men in a mist, seeking for freedom, and know not where, nor what it is: and those of the richer sort of you that see it, are ashamed and afraid to owne it, because it comes clothed in a clownish garment;... for freedom is the man that will turn the world upside downe, therefore no wonder he hath enemies...

"No true freedom can be established for Englands peace, or prove you faithfull in Covenant, but such a one as hath respect to the poor, as well as the rich; for if thou consent to freedom to the rich in the City, and givest freedome to the Free-holders in the Countrey, and to Priests and Lawyers, and Lords of Mannours, and Impropriators, and yet allowest the poor no freedome, thou art then a declared hypocrite." Winstanley had declared this truth to the Army (in the *Letter to the Lord Fairfax*) and Parliament (in *An Appeal to the House of Commons*), and "now you have all been spoken to... London, nay England, look to thy freedom; I'le assure thee, thou art very neere to be cheated of it, and if thou lose it now after all thy boasting, truly thy posterity will curse thee, for thy unfaithfulnesse to them: every one talks of freedome, but there are but few that act for freedome, and the actors for freedome are oppressed by the talkers and verball professors of freedome".

In the main body of the pamphlet, Winstanley includes the written statement he had submitted to the Kingston court. This begins with a blunt counter-charge that the whole proceedings are illegal on four counts: first, that the defendants were arrested without being given cause; second, that the court had twice refused to provide the defendants with copies of the

Declaration against them; third, that the court had denied them the right to put a defence except through a paid Attorney; and fourth, that in these circumstances the court had no right to proceed to judgment and execution. In insisting on his right to defend himself, without recourse to the lawyers he so despised, Winstanley was of course following in the footsteps of John Lilburne; and, like Lilburne, Winstanley was ready to quote chapter and verse of the law books to make a fool of the law: 36 Ed. this and 28 Ed. that, Coke's *Institutes*, the *Mirror of Justice*, and even *Magna Carta*.

Trespass was denied, since the trespass laws were "only an ancient custome, bred in the strength of Kingly Prerogative... which is of no force now to bind the people of England, since the Kingly power and office was cast out". Only the common people could limit common rights, and a court which dared to do so on the authority of the old regime, "they are Traytors to this Common-Wealth of England". The digging was justified as an action "to make the earth a common treasurie", which it was before the fall. For "the plain truth is, theeves and murderers, upheld by preaching witches and deceivers, rule the Nations: and for the present, the Laws and Government of the world, are Laws of darknesse, and the divells Kingdome, for covetousnesse rules all. And the power of the sword over brethren in Armies, in Arrests, in Prisons, in gallows, and in other inferiour torments, inflicted by some upon others, as the oppression of Lords of Mannours, hindring the poore from the use of the common Land, is Adam fallen".

England, however, had made a start in reversing the fall by replacing the "divells kingdome" with a commonwealth based on the National Covenant, "which the Parliament did make, of whom Mr Drake that caused us to be arrested was one". Winstanley warned the court that he had appealed to Parliament. "Therefore we hope you will do nothing rashly". He ended his highly unconventional plea in even more unusual style, with four lines of verse in the doggerel style of the times:

"Covetous might may overcome rationall right for a time,
But rationall right must conquer covetous might, and that's the life of mine.
The Law is righteous, just and good, when reason is the rule,
But who so rules by the fleshly will, declares himself a foole."

Since Winstanley saw the jury as "made of rich Free-holders, and such as stand strongly for the Norman power", he and his comrades cannot have been surprised by the verdicts brought against them. But it must have hurt them to hear of "the Lords Tenants" who "rode to the next Town shouting the diggers were conquered, the diggers were conquered". "Truly", he wrote, "it is an easie thing to beat a man, and cry conquest over him after his hands are tied, as they tyed ours". But the Diggers had their supporters. Before the bailiffs were forced to release the cattle they had seized from Winstanley's care, "strangers made rescue of those Cowes, and drove them astray... so that the Bailiffes lost them". It was a welcome act of solidarity, prefiguring similar acts by the kindly neighbours of Quakers a few years later when their animals were taken in lieu of tithes.

Winstanley refused to accept defeat. "I went away and left them, being quiet in my heart, and filled with comfort within my self, that the King of righteousnesse would cause this to work for the advancing of his own Cause... Saying likewise within my heart as I was walking along, O thou King of righteousnesse shew thy power, and do thy work thy self, and free thy people now from under this heavy bondage of miserie, Pharaoh the covetous power. And the answer in my heart was satisfactory, and full of sweet joy and peace: and so I said, Father, do what thou wilt, this cause is thine, and thou knowest that the love to righteousnesse makes me do what I do".

He concludes his pamphlet by asking: "Why are they so furious against us? but because we endeavour to dig up their Tythes, their Lawyers Fees, their Prisons, and all that Art and Trade of darknesse, whereby they get money under couller of Law". And if they are right, and Parliament confirms their law, "Then Souldiers where is the price of your bloud? and Countrey-men, and Citizens Where is the price of your Taxes and Free quarter?... And you zealous Preachers, and professors of the City of London and you great Officers and Souldiery of the Army, Where are all your Victories over the Cavaliers, that you made such a blaze in the Land, in giving God thanks for?... O thou City, thou Hypocriticall City! thou blindfold drowsie England, that sleps and snorts in the bed of covetousnesse, awake, awake, the Enemie is upon thy back, he is ready to scale the walls and enter the Possession, and wilt thou not look out?...

"I tell thee thou England, thy battells now are all spirituall. Dragon against the Lamb, and the power of love against the power of covetousnesse; therefore all that will be Souldiers for Christ, the Law of righteousnesse, joyn to the Lamb. He that takes the iron sword now shall perish with it, and would you be a strong Land and flourish in beauty, then fight the Lambs battels, and his strength shall be thy walls and bulwarks."

There is a final appeal to "you Knights, Gentlemen, and Freeholders, that sat in councell at the White Lion in Cobham to find out who are our backers", and particularly to Francis Drake. "You are a Parliament man, and was not the beginning of the quarrel between King Charles and your House?... This the King pleaded to uphold Prerogative, and you were against it, and yet must a Parliament man be the first man to uphold Prerogative?... Did you not promise liberty to the whole Nation, in case the Cavalier party were cast out? And why now wil you seek liberty to your self and Gentry, with the deniall of just liberty and freedome to the common people, that have born the greatest burden?"

That was the key question at that stage of the English revolution. With the benefit of hindsight, we know the answers. They were not Gerrard Winstanley's answers.

Winstanley's parallel *Appeal to the House of Commons* also recounted the proceedings in the Kingston court and asked Parliament bluntly "Whether the common people, after all their taxes, free-quarter, and loss of blood to recover England from under the Norman yoak, shal have the freedom to improve the Comons, and waste Lands free to themselves... Or whether the Lords of Manors shall have them, according to the old Custom from the Kings Will and Grant, and so remain Task-Masters still over us". No doubt Winstanley knew the formal answer. Although England was now a republic (the Commons finally declared it a "free commonwealth" on May 19), Parliament had passed two Acts within days of Charles's execution authorising Justices and other royal officials to continue until new commissions were issued, and permitting action under the old laws in the name of "the Keepers of the Liberty of England" in place of the king. But these were supposed to be temporary provisions pending a permanent settlement of such questions. It was time for the permanent settlement, Winstanley argued, and the "Keepers of the Liberty of England" were called upon to justify their grand title. "We have made our appeal to you, to settle this matter in the Equity and Reason of it, and to pass the sentence of freedom to us, you being the men with whom we have to do in this business, in whose hands there is power to settle it, for no Court can end this controversie but your Court of Parliament."

The Norman yoke is again invoked as the origin of all the oppressions to which the native English have been subject. It is Parliament's duty to complete its task of breaking the yoke. "You called upon us to assist you with plate, taxes, freequarter, and our persons; and you promised us, in the name of the Almighty, to make us a free people; thereupon you and we took the National Covenant with joynt consent, to endeavour the freedom, peace and safety of the people of England...

"And seeing in particular you swore to endeavour the freedom, peace and safety of this people of England, shutting out no sort from freedom; therefore you cannot say that the Gentry and Clergy were only comprehended, but without exception, all sorts of people in the land are to have freedom, seeing all sorts have assisted you in person and purse, and the common people more especially, seeing their estates were weakest, and their misery in the wars the greatest.

"Therefore let the Gentry and Freeholders have their inclosures freed from all entanglements of Fines, Heriots, and other burdens, and let the common people have their Commons and waste lands freed from the entanglements of the Norman Lords of Mannors, and pluck up all Norman Tyranny by the roots, and so keep your Covenant... but if you will not, you give a just occasion to the common people of England, never to trust the fair words of a Parliament any more."

In another telling thrust, Winstanley reminds Parliament that it had not been slow to abolish ancient duties owed by the gentry to the king. Royal fines had been abolished, as had the royal privileges exercised through the old Court of Wards and Liveries. So, "seeing you took away the will of the King from enslaving Lords of Mannors, Take away the will of Lords of Mannors from enslaving the Common People".

The *Appeal* ends with a summary of "some of the Norman laws which William the Conqueror brought into England". The Normans and their royal successors had "turned the English out of their Lands" and divided them among barons and lords of manors; caused the laws to be written in French so that the English would have to pay Norman lawyers to plead their cause; and "brought in the paying of Tithes to the Clergy" to encourage priests to persuade the people to obey their masters.

The Kingdom's Faithfull Scout, *The Moderate Messenger*, *The Moderate Intelligencer* and *The Perfect Weekly Account* all reported that the *Appeal* was presented to the House on July 24. But Winstanley cannot have expected any meaningful debate, let alone positive action. His aim was maximum publicity, and this he achieved both by printing and disseminating his letters and appeals as pamphlets and by getting the Diggers' arguments, as well as their actions, reported in the national press. The radicals had found a publicist without peer. The man who memorably wrote that "words and writings were all nothing" compared with action was brilliantly demonstrating in action that words and writings had their vital, creative and inspirational place in the Lamb's war against the Dragon.

VIII
Enter Parson Platt

The George's Hill colony had survived for four months. It had suffered repeated attacks by mobs, soldiers, clergy and the gentry's courts. Its seeds had been uprooted, its corn trampled, its huts and shelters pulled to the ground, its tools stolen or wrecked, its carts cut to pieces, its one horse disabled. But its numbers had slowly risen to fifty or more men, plus women and children. A second Digger colony may also have been established by this time in Iver, Buckinghamshire, and another in Wellingborough, Northamptonshire, with more appearing sporadically over the next year. Parliament, the Army Council and the City of London had all had the True Levellers' cause brought to their attention. The press had run with a story which proved to have legs. Just as "official" Levelling seemed to be on the wane, its schismatic offspring offered hope that freedom might yet prove to be the man that would turn the world upside down.

But at the height of the summer, Winstanley and his followers suddenly abandoned George's Hill. It has been conjectured that they felt forced by the Kingston judgment to move off Drake's jurisdiction, or that the repeated attacks had ruined the settlement, or that they judged the heathland too barren for successful cultivation. For whatever reason, they moved just over a mile away to land on Cobham heath, where it seems a group of them had already planted a crop of barley a few weeks earlier. The new settlement was over the Walton border and the lord of the manor of Cobham was the local parson, John Platt, who had taken possession on his marriage into the Lynde family which had owned it.

In view of Platt's later implacable hostility to the Diggers, it will seem odd to suggest that the move into his territory may have been made in the expectation that he would prove a sympathetic landlord. Platt was no episcopalian churchman: he had been a member of the Guildford Presbyterian "classis" and a "trier" for Surrey, which gave him good Puritan and Parliamentary credentials. After the Restoration, he was to be ejected from his living for nonconformity. Winstanley may have judged that Platt would leave the colony undisturbed. If so, he was cruelly mistaken.

Within days of their move, a meeting was called in Cobham's White Lion inn of local gentry and freeholders, "to advise together" (as Winstanley wrote in *A Watch-word to the City of London*) "what course they should take to subdue the diggers; for, say they, if the cause of the diggers stand, we shall lose all our honour and titles" and be reduced to the level of servants. No action appears to have been taken, however, till October 16, when the newspapers reported "a Petty Insurrection at Cobham" involving about 50 Diggers, perhaps the result of an attempted eviction. *Mercurius Elenctitus* reported that the design of the insurrectionists was "to levell all things... and to introduce a new frame of Government" committed to a real commonwealth, by which the Diggers meant "a Community in all things".

Shortly after, Parson Platt and a delegation of gentlemen and justices reported to Fairfax and the Council of State that (as Winstanley put it in his own *Letter to my Lord Generall*), the Cobham diggers were "a riotous people, and that wee will not be ruled by the Justices, and that we hold a mans house by violence from him, and that we have 4 guns in it, to secure ourselves, and that we are drunkards, and Cavaleers waiteing an opportunity to helpe to bringe in the Prince, and such like". The "such like" included dark hints that the colony's community of land and goods included community of women. The Council was divided in its response. A suggestion that a troop of horse be sent to the heath was met with the counter-suggestion that matters be left to the local quarter sessions. Platt, it seems, refused to leave Whitehall till some action was agreed on, and after a fortnight of his persistent lobbying the Council agreed to despatch troops, if only to get the belligerent parson off their backs. Fairfax, however, still convinced that the Diggers were harmless eccentrics rather than free-booting, free-loving insurrectionists, and mindful of his earlier promises, insisted that the soldiers' mission was to protect the Sheriff and Justices, and not to attack the colonists.

Such niceties would not deter Parson Platt. On November 27 he rode to Cobham heath with the Sheriff, Justices, soldiers and tenants. The soldiers, says Winstanley, were "very moderate and rationall", but Platt commanded his tenants to pull down one of the Diggers' houses, which they "durst do no other... for fear they should be turned out of service, or their livings", while Platt and his fellow landlords "rejoyced with shouting at the fall". Platt wanted a second house destroyed, but the Sheriff apparently demurred. Next day, Platt sent two soldiers and three of his tenants to complete the work in the Sheriff's absence. Again there is evidence of some unease at the parson's violence. "One of these souldiers was very civill, and walked lovingly with the Diggers round their corn which they had planted, and commended the work, and would do no harm (as divers others were of the same minde) and when he went his way gave the Diggers 12d. to drink: but the other souldier was so rude, that he forced those three Country-men to help him to pull down the house, and railed bitterly: the men were unwilling to pull it down; but for fear of their Landlords, and the threatning souldier, they did put their hands to pull it down". As a result, they "turned a poor old man and his wife and daughter out of doors to lie in the field in a cold night".

The Diggers offered no resistance. Their rule of non-violence had evidently taken deep root. Instead, writes Winstanley in *A New-yeers Gift*, they were "very chearfull, and preached the Gospel to those Turkish Bashaws" [pashas, or warlords]. When their persecutors left, they made "little Hutches to lie in like Calf-cribs, and are cheerful; taking the spoyling of their goods patiently, and rejoycing that they are counted worthy to suffer persecution for Righteousnesse sake: and they follow their work close, and have Planted divers Acres of Wheat and Rie, which is come up and promises a very fruitful crop, and Resolves to preserve it by all the diligence they can, and nothing shall make them slack but want of Food, which is not much now, they all being poor People, and having suffered so much in one expence or other since they began; for Poverty is their greatest burthen; and if anything do break them from the Work, it will be that".

Winstanley hurried into print two more pamphlets publicising the actions of their persecutors and answering the rumours Platt had spread about them. The first was *Two Letters to Lord Fairfax*, written in December, one signed by John Heyman and six other Diggers (but not Winstanley), the other by Winstanley himself. The first asks Fairfax to "call your souldiers to accompt for attempting to abuse us with your commission, that the Cuntry may know that you had no hand in such an unrighteous and cruell act". Winstanley's own letter *To my Lord Generall and his Councell of Warr* mocks Platt's charges that the Diggers are a bunch of armed drunken Cavaliers, and counter-charges that the gentry who are persecuting them were themselves old royalists who had "had a hand in the Kentish rising, and were cheife promotors of the offensive Surry petition" - two recent examples of last-ditch royalist resistance.

Both letters were short and to the point. Winstanley reserved his full rebuttal of Platt for a more detailed account of the events at Cobham, published on January 1 1650 as *A New-yeers Gift for the Parliament and Armie* - his thirteenth pamphlet in less than two years, and his ninth specifically communist work. He again mocks the absurd charge that the

Diggers are secret Cavaliers plotting to restore the crown, that they have stolen sheep, geese and pigs from their neighbours, and that they "hold women to be common, and live in bestialnesse". "For my part", he says of this latter charge, "I declare against it; I own this to be a truth, that the earth ought to be a common Treasury to all; but as for women, *Let every man have his own wife, and every woman her own husband*; and I know none of the Diggers that act in such unrationall excesse of female communitie: If any should, I professe to have nothing to do with such people, but leave them to their own Master, who will pay them with torment of minde, and diseases in their bodies." Not for the last time, as we shall see, Winstanley wished to make clear that he was no Ranter, and, indeed, no critic of conventional Puritan sexual mores.

The whole pamphlet, in three distinct parts, burns with indignation, but insists (sometimes with an air of desperate determination) that the Diggers will bear persecution cheerfully and without resistance. With the Reverend John Platt evidently much in mind, Winstanley returns in the first part to his earlier attacks on the hypocrisy of church and churchmen. "It is true indeed, they are spiritual; but it is of the spiritual power of Covetousness and Pride; for the spiritual power of Love and Righteousness they know not... The Clergie will serve on any side, like our ancient Laws, that will serve any Master: They will serve the Papists, they will serve the Protestants, they will serve the King, they will serve the States". And the clergy are not the only religious hypocrites. "O ye rulers of England, you make a blazing profession, That you know, and that you own God, Christ, and the Scriptures: but did Christ ever declare such hardness of heart? did not he bid the rich man go and sell all that he hath and give to the Poor? and does not the Scripture say, If thou makest a Covenant, keep it?... If you own God, Christ and Scripture, now make Restitution, and deliver us quiet possession of our Land."

Winstanley declares boldly that it is the Diggers, not the priests, who observe true religion. "Sirs, Though your Tithing Priests and others tell you, That we Diggers do deny God, Christ, and the Scripture, to make us odious, and themselves better thought of; yet you will see in time when the King of Righteousness whom we serve does cleer our innocencie, That our actions and conversation is the very life of the Scripture, and holds forth the true power of God and Christ. For is not the end of all preaching, praying, and profession wrapped up in this action, namely, *Love your enemies, and doe to all men, as you would they should do to you, for this is the very Law and the Prophets*. This is the New Commandement that Christ left behind him. Now if any seem to say this, and does not do this, but acts contrary, for my part I owne not their wayes, they are members that uphold the curse. Bare talking of righteousnesse, and not acting, hath ruled, and yet does rule king of darkness in the creation; and it is the cause of all this immoderate confusion and ignorance that is in men."

Winstanley has his own clear vision of "true religion":

"True Religion, and undefiled, is this, To make restitution of the Earth, which hath been taken and held from the Common people... The Land... was made for all; and true Religion is, To let every one enjoy it. Therefore, you Rulers of England, make restitution of the Lands which the Kingly power holds from us: *Set the oppressed free*; and come in, and honour Christ, who is the Restoring Power, and you shall finde rest."

The second part of *A New-yeers Gift*, entitled *The Curse and the Blessing that is in Mankinde*, begins with a reversion to Winstanley's earlier style of theological imagery. Happy to use the clergy's own language, Winstanley always gave it his own spin. *Curse and... Blessing* begins with a powerful restatement of Winstanley's panentheism: "In the beginning of Time, the Spirit of Universal Love appeared to be the father of all things: the Creation of Fire, Water, Earth, and Air, came out of him, and is his clothing. *Love* is the *Word*." When this Spirit of universal Love is allowed to "rule king" in mankind, "this Earth is then in peace, and is grown up to the perfection of a man annointed. But when Self or Particular Love rules, which is called the sin of Covetousness, then this Earth is brought into Bondage, and Sorrow fills all places. This is the dark side of the Cloud, in which there is no true peace." Love as "the father of all things" had made the earth "a common Treasury of livelihood to whole mankind without respect of persons" - and, he adds, "for all other creatures likewise". But alongside universal Love, which is "the power of Light" and reason, is "the power of Darkness, which is particular self love, and this is called the Curse". It is the Curse that now "rules King in the Earth... for this power hath filled all places, with his stinking self seeking Government, and troubles every body".

But the blessing, the reign of love and light, is not some future event to be patiently and passively awaited. It is to be enacted by those who reject the curse, the fall. And again Winstanley insists that this new kingdom is not to be won by force of arms and the exercise of power. "For my part, and the rest [of the Diggers]... we abhor fighting for Freedom, it is acting of the

Curse and lifting him up higher; and do thou uphold it by the Sword, we will not; we will conquer by Love and Patience, or else we count it no Freedom: Freedom gotten by the Sword is an established Bondage to some part or other of the Creation; and this we have Declared publickly enough... Victory that is gotten by the Sword, is a Victory that slaves gets one over another;... but Victory obtained by Love, is a Victory for a King".

The True Levellers are allied with the Spirit and "his inward power of love, light, and righteousnes... This great Leveller, Christ our King of righteousness in us, shall cause men to beat their swords into plowshares, and spears into pruning hooks, and nations shall learn war no more, and every one shall delight to let each other enjoy the pleasures of the earth, and shall hold each other no more in bondage; then what will become of your power? truly he must be cast out for a murtherer; and I pittie you for the torment your spirit must go through, if you be not fore-armed, as you are abundantly forewarned from all places; but I look upon you as part of the creation who must be restored, and the Spirit may give you wisedom to foresee a danger, as he hath admonished divers of your rank already to leave those high places, and to lie quiet and wait for the breakings forth of the powerful day of the Lord. Farewel, once more. Let Israel go free."

The third part is a short postscript, described as "A bill of account of the most remarkable sufferings that the Diggers have met with from the great red Dragons power since April 1. 1649". Each attack on the colony, first at George's Hill and then at Cobham Heath, is listed briefly in a model of the "sufferings" records soon to be collected and published regularly by the Quakers. There is an unmistakable note of resignation and valediction in the closing passages: "Gentlemen of the Army, we have spoken to you, we have appealed to the Parliament, we have declared our cause in all humilitie to you all, and we are Englishmen, and your friends that stuck to you in your miseries, and these Lords of Mannors that oppose us were wavering on both sides, yet you have heard them, and answered their request to beat us off, and yet you would not afford us an Answer.

"Yet love and patience shall lie down and suffer; Let pride and covetousness stretch themselves upon their beds of ease, and forget the afflictions of Joseph, and persecute us for righteousness sake, yet we will wait to see the issue, the power of righteousness is our God; the globe runs round, the longest Sun-shine day ends in a dark night; and therefore to thee O thou King of righteousness we doe commit our cause; Judge thou between us and them that strive against us, and those that deal treacherously with thee and us, and doe thine own work, and help weak flesh in whom the Spirit is willing."

At the start of 1650, Winstanley has come to a clear sense that he can do no more than he has done. "And here I end, having put my Arm as far as my strength will go to advance Righteousness: I have Writ, I have Acted, I have Peace: and now I must wait to see the Spirit do his own work in the hearts of others, and whether England shall be the first Land, or some other, wherein Truth shall sit down in triumph."

IX
The Rant

Winstanley was nothing if not prolific with his pen. Platt would have done better to have seized his stock of writing paper. That December he saw through Calvert's press a reprint with revisions of all his first five pamphlets, in a single volume. At around the same time he must have been working on the second, slightly revised, edition of *Truth Lifting Up its Head Above Scandals*, which appeared in the new year. And within the same short period (the precise dating is uncertain) he produced *Englands Spirit Unfoulded, or an Incouragment to take the Engagement*. We are reminded that there was now a growing demand for his works. Winstanley had his own reading public.

But in the winter months of 1649/50 the Diggers had other troubles than those inflicted by Parson Platt and his cronies. In *A New-yeers Gift* Winstanley had acknowledged - and denied - the rumour that the Diggers were practising "community of women" as well as land. In this case, however, it seems that the smoke really did signal fire. What had apparently happened was that some who had joined the colony were associated with or influenced by a group known as the Ranters, some of whose leaders openly preached and practised sexual freedom and open marriage. Already pariahs for their unorthodox religious views and actions, the Diggers now faced the prospect of further alienation from their respectable neighbours and potential supporters by association with scandal.

The Ranters were never an organised sect or association (and should not be confused with the very different Methodist evangelical Ranters of a later century). Nor did those who were called Ranters by their enemies, or adopted the name as a defiant badge of honour, have any coherent body of beliefs, religious, political or social. The movement, if it can be called such, was prominent from 1649 to 1651, and at its height as the Diggers were seeking recruits. It receded after the introduction of the 1650 Blasphemy Act, and some Ranters joined the new radical movements of the fifties - the Quakers, Muggletonians and Fifth Monarchists.

It was not uncommon for radically unorthodox groups to be accused by their respectable neighbours of sexual licence. The Family of Love before the Ranters, and the Quakers after, suffered dark hints that their meetings for worship included disrobing, sensual dancing or group sex, perhaps because both groups gave women freedom to minister, a practice that seemed unnatural and provocative to the male puritan psyche. The occasional Quaker practice of "going naked as a sign" must have encouraged such suspicions. But in the case of the Ranters, or at least some of them, the accusations were true and openly admitted.

Ranters were at the outer extremity of "antinomianism", the doctrine that no "outward law" or commandment was binding on the redeemed. To the pure, all things were pure. Christ had redeemed us from sin: therefore sin was no more: therefore no action was sinful. Lawrence Clarkson, an Anglican-turned-Presbyterian-turned-Baptist-turned-Seeker, was the most prominent of the Ranters who preached this doctrine, which had obvious appeal to lusty young men and unconventional young women, newly liberated by the revolution from the constraints of puritan clergy and moral overseers. Clarkson wrote in a book called *A Single Eye*, widely-read at the time as a result of the denunciations which poured from pulpits and the respectable presses, that "there is no such act as drunkenness, adultery and theft in God... Sin hath its conception only in the imagination... What act soever is done by thee in light and love, is light and lovely, though it be that act called adultery... No matter what Scripture, saints or churches say, if that within thee do not condemn thee, thou shalt not be condemned". And no-one could accuse him of failing to practise what he preached, travelling as he did, sometimes with Mrs Clarkson, sometimes with a Mrs Star or a Mrs Middleton, once tangling with a "maid of pretty knowledge, who with my doctrine was affected", recalling fondly an occasion when "Dr Paget's maid stripped herself naked and skipped" at a Ranter meeting, and generally giving his body to other women in light and lovely manner as the spirit moved him[1].

Clarkson evidently brushed with Winstanley, probably visiting him at Cobham heath, for he claims in *A Single Eye* that he told Winstanley "there was self-love and vain-glory nursed in his heart", and that his object in digging was "to have gained people to him, by which his name might become great among the poor Commonalty of the nation". Clarkson may have visited with other Ranters, some of whom stayed or made converts. However that may be, Winstanley's next two pamphlets roundly condemned Ranting and sought to dissociate the Diggers from such practices.

Probably the first of the two to appear was *Englands Spirit Unfoulded*, where the attack on the Ranters appears as a postscript tacked on to the main text. The postscript, entitled "A Watch-Word", begins with a few lines of doggerel verse which may have been Winstanley's own or may have been drawn from a current broadside ballad:

"Beware you Women of the ranting crew
And call not freedom those things which are vaine,
For if a child you get, by ranting deeds
The man is gone and leaves the child your gaine,
Then you and yours are left by such free-men,
For other women are as free for them."

Winstanley continues: "This is to certifie that, if any of the Diggers fall into the practice of Ranting, they fall off from their principles, as some in all Churches does". Ranting is "the Golden, pleasing, and deceitful baite whereby the foolish young man is taken, ensnared, and wrapped up into many bondages. It is a nursury of idleness, hardness of heart and hipocrisie, making men to speak one thing and do another, that they may injoy their destroying delights... It is the Kingdom of Satan... It is the resurrection of the unclean, boggish darke power, which is called the wicked man, or the Devill." Parson Platt could hardly have expressed his revulsion more plainly.

We shall return to the question of the precise dating of *Englands Spirit* when we consider its main text, but it seems clear that it preceded publication of *A Vindication of those, whose Endeavors is only to make the Earth a Common Treasury, called Diggers*, which carries the date February 20 1650 and a postscript dated March 4. Subtitled "Some Reasons given by them against the immoderate use of creatures, or the excessive community of women, called Ranting; or rather Renting", it treats more fully and with greater urgency the theme of the "Watch-Word" tacked on to *Englands Spirit*. (Winstanley's play with Ranting/Renting is presumably a pun intended to suggest the commodification of sex: prostitution).

The *Vindication* does not quarrel with the Ranters' supposed social doctrines, many of which were close to those Winstanley and the Diggers espoused, but with their practice of sexual freedom and eating and drinking in excess, condemned again as "the Devills Kingdome of darknesse". Both kinds of excess are "destructive to the body"and bring "vexation to the mind". Sexual licence in particular "breaks the peace in Families", "spills the seed in vaine, and... produces weaknesse and much infirmnesse, through immoderate heat". It is "the resurrection of the uncleane doggish beastly nature... the filthy, unrighteous power in all its branches". (As G E Aylmer noted[2], the use of the word "doggish" here suggests that what is printed as "boggish" in the earlier "Watch-Word", is probably a misprint though which of the two words is the more appropriately colourful is hard to say). It has generally been assumed that Winstanley is speaking from direct and bitter experience of the damage done within his community by Ranters when he condemns them for "the wastfull spending of the Treasures of the Earth". But as the passage continues, with Winstanley attributing to Ranting the "Anger, rage and varietie of vexations [which] possesses the mind, and inflames their harts to quarrelling, killing, burning houses or Corne, or to such like distructivenesse", we might wonder whether it is his persecutors rather than deviants within his own community that he has in mind or wishes his readers to have in mind.

In a remarkable and very Winstanleyan passage, however, he argues against the prosecution and punishment of Ranters. "Let none goe about to suppresse that ranting power by their punishing hand, for it is the work of the Righteous and rational spirit within, not thy hand without which must suppresse it; But if thou wilt needs be punishing: Then see thou be without sinne thy selfe, and then cast the first Stone at the Ranter; Let not sinners punish others for sin, but let the power of thy Reason and righteous action, shame and so beat downe their unrationall actings. Would thou live in peace; Then look to thy own wayes, mind thy owne Kingdome within, trouble not at the unrational government of other mens kingdomes without; Let every one alone, to stand and fall to their owne Master." Parson Platt could hardly have written *this* paragraph!

It must not be supposed that Winstanley's concern for the reputation and good moral standing of the Diggers so preoccupied him at this period that he lost contact with the wider politics which framed the action of digging and his enaction of community. While the postscript to *Englands Spirit Unfoulded* deals with Ranting, the main pamphlet itself has a far wider national political focus. It was lost and entirely unknown until G E Aylmer discovered what is still the only known copy among the Clarke Papers at Worcester College, Oxford, and published the text in 1968[3]. Unusually, it was not printed by Calvert but by one "W.L" (Aylmer suggests William Larner). It is undated, but both its principal subject-matter and the postscript on Ranting date it to the winter of 1649/50, and probably January or February. This is the same time that Winstanley was preoccupied with the *Two Letters to Lord Fairfax* and the *New Yeers Gift for the Parliament and*

Armie, which may well explain why he had to go to a different printer. In the event, "W.L" did a poor job. *Englands Spirit* has more than the common number of uncorrected mistakes, which may well betray Winstanley's own haste, with so much to be done and so little time in which to do it.

As indicated by its sub-title - "An Incouragement to take the Engagement" - it is a polemic on the single most critical issue which divided England over those winter months. February 1649 had seen the republican regime introduce a loyalty oath of "Engagement" to be taken by members of the first Council of State. In the autumn, a revised "New Engagement" was required of all MPs and other office-holders under the Commonwealth, and in the winter it was extended to the entire adult male population. No-one could escape the necessity of either taking the Engagement and declaring for the regime, or refusing to do so and thereby aligning themselves with the opposition. The Independents campaigned furiously for, the Presbyterians and old royalists against. Radical left-wing groups like the Levellers were divided, some seeing the regime, despite its evident weaknesses, as the necessary foundation for further advance, while others declared it already beyond reformation. A few opposed the Engagement because they were against a loyalty oath in principle. And some, like John Lilburne, equivocated. Aylmer suggests that Lilburne's support for the Engagement was "tongue in cheek" in that his only reason for taking it was to enable him to be a common councilman of the City of London (from which position he was in any case immediately ejected).

The discovery of *Englands Spirit Unfoulded* makes it clear beyond any shadow of doubt that, despite his radical criticism of what he saw as the barely-half-way stance of the regime, and in spite of the hostility and persecution he and his comrades had suffered and were then suffering at the hands of the state, Winstanley threw himself wholeheartedly behind the Engagement. At this point, at least, he is in no doubt that, for all its faults and shortcomings, for all its reluctance to follow its despatch of the king with an equally definitive rejection of "Norman" kingly governance, and despite its avowed contempt for any notion of the earth as a common treasury, the republican government at Whitehall was the only possible basis for further social advance. Although the same stance is implicit in *A New Yeers Gift to the Parliament and Armie*, the *Two Letters to Fairfax* and the later *Appeale to all Englishmen*, *Englands Spirit Unfoulded* is the one political pamphlet in which Winstanley campaigns openly and unequivocally for the Government. As Aylmer comments, "It deals with one of the great and universal issues of obligation and allegiance: what support should the man of principle give to a regime which contains some of the prerequisites for bringing about the juster social order which he desires, but at the same time is characterized by backsliding and human frailty?" Radicals under New Labour will recognise the problem as one that will not go away.

The form of *Englands Spirit* is unusual for Winstanley, though common enough among broadsides of the period. Winstanley pitches it as "a salutary Discourse between two Friends", one of whom, *A*, asks the kind of questions about the Engagement which could no doubt be heard on any street corner or in any alehouse, while the other, *O*, provides Winstanley's pro-Engagement answers. The dialogue is prefaced by one of Winstanley's verses:

"Freedom is the mark, at which all men should aime
But what true freedom is, few men doth know by name,
But now a light is rise [riz], and nere shall fall
How every man by name, shall freedom call."

A begins by asking what people are saying about the Engagement. *O* assures him that "the generality of people like it well", as it makes good the two Acts abolishing the office of king and declaring the people of England a Commonwealth and a free state. But, *A* asks, "may not parliament prove as tyrannical as Lords and King?" "No", replies *O*, because parliament-men can be turned out at elections. They must do as the people wish to retain their places. He assures *A* that this view is shared "by all unbyassed men, that loves England's freedom". Who opposes it? Lords of manors, tithing priests, impropriators, lawyers, "Covetous Usurers" and landlords. These "would be free-men themselves, but they would have all others bondmen".

In the passage where Winstanley's arguments for the Engagement are most distinctively his own, he suggests that, properly understood and honoured, it will give men and women "freedom... to go build and plant upon the Common Land". Oddly, this crucial passage is put in the mouth of the questioner *A* rather than *O* - evidently a printer's error which, repeated more than once, did nothing to clarify the pamphlet's argument. But what is quite clear is that, in the winter of 1649/50, and despite the desperation of his own situation, Winstanley believed that Christ was to rise in and through the revolutionary regime, not in spite of it. The Council of State was the agency by which Reason would deliver freedom, not the obstacle and enemy to freedom it had seemed when Winstanley wrote *The True Levellers Standard Advanced* and *Truth Lifting up its Head above Scandals*, and would seem again only a few months later.

But it was the Ranting charge that was giving Winstanley his most immediate problems, and he soon had another reason for distancing Diggers from Ranters. In the postscript he added in March to his *Vindication*, he says he has been "told there are some people goes up and downe in the Country among such as are friends to the Diggers gathering Moneyes in their name. And they have a note wherein my name and divers others are subscribed." He has never subscribed his name to any such note. "Neither have we that are called Diggers received any money by any such Collections." Although he does not name them, he clearly supposes these "Cheats" to be Ranters. Supporters are asked to send contributions "by some trustie friend".

If Winstanley had subscribed his name to "no such note" in March, he had certainly put his name to an appeal by April. Perhaps the reported success of the Ranters in fraudulently raising money in the colony's name encouraged him to send out his own genuine emissaries and fund-raisers. It is clear that, after another bad winter, the Cobham heath settlement was desperately short of food, shelter, tools and money to pay for them. Accordingly, Winstanley appointed two Diggers, Thomas Heaydon and Adam Knight, to travel the country with an appeal letter signed by Winstanley and 21 others. The colony seems to have halved in size since the autumn, though Winstanley adds, after the 21 names, "Besides their Wives and Children, and many more if there were food for them".

The letter reported that, despite losing the previous summer's work "in regard of the great opposition hitherto from the enemy... they keep the field still and have planted divers Acres of Corn and built 4 houses, and now this season time goes on digging, endeavouring to plant as much as they can; but in regard of poverty their work is like to flagge and droppe". Money is urgently required "to buy Victualls to keep the men alive, and to buy Corn to cast into the ground". This is needed to "keep alive the beginning of publique Freedom to the whole Land, which otherwise is ready to die again for want of help;

"And if you hear hereafter that there was a people appeared to stand up to advance publique freedome, and strugled with the opposing power of the Land for that they begin to let them alone, and yet these men and their publique work was crushed, because they wanted assistance of food and Corne to keep them alive; I say if you heare this it will be a trouble to you when it is too late, that you had monies in your hands, and would not part with any of it to purchase freedome, therefore you deservedly Grone under Tyranny and no Saviour appeares; but let your Reason weigh the excellency of this worke of digging the Commons, and I am sure you will cast in something."

The letter ends with a warning against the "treacherous persons" who had been collecting on false pretences. Winstanley did not publish it himself, but Heaydon, Knight and two men with them were apprehended at Wellingborough and the letter was leaked to one of the news-sheets, *A Perfect Diurnall*, which printed it under a report that the men were "going about to incite people to digging, and under that pretence gathered mony of the Wel-affected for their assistance". The paper included "a Copy of their travels that were taken with the four men", which showed them to have journeyed "out of Buckinghamshire into Surry, from Surry to Middlesex, from thence to Hartfordshire, to Bedfordshire, again to Buckinghamshire, so to Barkeshire, and then to Surry, thence to Middlesex, and so to Hartfordshire, and to Bedfordshire, thence into Huntingdonshire, from thence to Bedfordshire, and so into Northamptonshire, and there they were Apprehended."

The towns visited "to promote the Businesse" were named: "Colebrook, Hanworth, Hounslow, Harrowhill, Watford, Redburn, Dunstable, Barton, Amersley, Bedford, Kempson, North Crawly, Cranfield, Newport, Stony-Stratford, Winslow, Wendover, Wickham, Windsor, Cobham, London, Whetstone, Mine, Wellin, Dunton, Putney, Royston, St Needs, Godmanchester, Wetne, Stanton, Warbays, Kimolton, Wellingborow."

Christopher Hill, in *The World Turned Upside Down*, has figured out a pattern in this to-ing and fro-ing. That spring had seen new Diggers' colonies, or embryonic communities, begun at Colnbrook, Hounslow Heath, Harrow-on-the-Hill and Dunstable, and in Barnet, Enfield and Hampstead, perhaps subsumed in the list under "Middlesex" and "London". Another colony had just been established at Wellingborough, where the messengers were apprehended, and had published its own manifesto on March 12. Fenstanton ("Stanton") and Warboys had Baptist congregations founded by the Leveller leader Henry Denne, and Winstanley seems to have had connections and sympathisers in Hertfordshire. The colony at Iver, Buckinghamshire, had existed for nearly a year. There is some evidence for another colony in Nottinghamshire, and Winstanley himself is said to have "invaded" Fenny Drayton in the neighbouring county of Leicestershire, where he disputed with George Fox's former minister, Nathaniel Stephens.

It seems clear that the Cobham heath community had started to become a mother-settlement to others, short-lived as they were, and that Winstanley's emissaries were targeting places where there were known to be sympathisers, if not active Diggers. There were other colonies or sympathisers in Gloucestershire, Kent and Essex. Hill comments, perhaps with some exaggeration, that "from Nottinghamshire and Northamptonshire to Gloucestershire and Kent, Digger influence spread all over southern and central England".

On March 26, a week before his missionaries were arrested, Winstanley issued his sixteenth pamphlet, *An Appeale to all Englishmen*, evidently to encourage the new ventures which were springing up. Its argument is that digging is warranted not only by scripture but by the new laws of England, specifically those abolishing monarchy and declaring a Commonwealth. "The Land of England now is your free Inheritance: all Kingly and Lordly entanglements are declared against, by our Army and Parliament. The Norman power is beaten in the field, and his head is cut off: And that oppressing Conquest that hath raigned over you by King and House of Lords, for about 600 yeares past, is now cast out, by the Armies Swords, the Parliaments Acts and Lawes, and the Common-wealths Engagement." All that remained was for the people to claim their lawful inheritance. "Come, those that are free within, turn your Swords into Plough-shares, and Speares into pruning-hookes, and take Plow and Spade, and break up the Common Land, build you Houses, sow Corne, and take possession of your own Land."

Again, action is the life of all. "For it is the badge of hypocrisie, for a man to say, and not do. Therefore we leave this with you all, having peace in our hearts, by declaring faithfully to you, this light that is in us, and which we do not onley speake and write, but which we do easily act & practise. Likewise we write it as a Letter of congratulation, and encouragement to our dear fellow Englishmen, that have begun to digge upon the Commons, thereby taking possession of their freedom in Willinborow [Wellingborough], in Northamptonshire: And at Cox Hall in Kent [it has been suggested that this is a mistake for Coggeshall in Essex], waiting to see the chains of slavish fear to break and fall off from the hearts of others in other Countries [counties], till at last the whole Land is filled with the knowledge & righteousness of restoring power, which is Christ himself, Abrahams seed, who will spread himself til he become the joy of all Nations." The work is signed by Winstanley and twenty-four others, "and divers... that were not present when this went to the Presse".

The indefatigable pamphleteer already had at least one other work in preparation. Winstanley had had a meeting with Parson Platt where, he says, "Mr Plat did promise and engage himself with loving expressions, and words savouring of much moderation, tenderness and reason, that if Gerard Winstanly could prove by Scriptures, the lawfulnesse of the work, that is, that the earth was made a common Treasury, and ought to remain so to whole Mankind, without respect of persons: That he would never hereafter molest the Diggers, but quietly suffer them to build and plant the Commons in his Lordship: And that he would bring in his Estate, and become one in that community". Accordingly, Winstanley set out his own interpretation of the scriptures, ostensibly for Mr Platt, dating his opening address April 9 and publishing it a few weeks later as his seventeenth pamphlet, *An Humble Request to the Ministers of Both Universities and to all Lawyers in Every Inns-a-Court*. It marshalls all the relevant biblical texts, but its greatest interest lies in the account Winstanley added of Platt's own response: one of action rather than textual exegesis, as we shall see.

For Platt too, in a very different sense from Winstanley's, action spoke louder than words.

X
The rout

April 1650 began as Chaucer's sweet month, and ended as Eliot's cruellest. The long dark night of winter was over, the heath was blossoming, and the annual miracle of resurrection promised new life and hope. Winstanley seems to have seen off his Ranters, restoring domestic harmony to his colony and consolidating his own leadership. The number of acres under corn had grown to eleven, and the four houses built over the winter to replace the "hutch-like cribs" which had been their only shelter after the November attacks had now doubled to eight. The colony was still critically short of tools, money and food, but there seemed good prospects that the scheme of collections would soon remedy this. Above all, evidence that digging the commons was beginning to spread must have greatly raised spirits and revived confidence that the Christ of Reason and the universal Spirit of Love were indeed on the rise. Perhaps, too, the sweet-talking of Parson Platt, his apparent willingness to study the scriptural proof-texts Winstanley had dug out for him, even to the point of saying he would join the colony and throw in his whole estate if he lost the argument, made for a new hope that what had been begun in April 1649 would prove irresistible in April 1650.

Such hopes were quickly dashed. As Easter week approached, Platt and Thomas Sutton, the lay impropriator of Cobham church, led a party of hired men to Cobham heath to demolish all the new buildings. A house was pulled down and the family in it attacked, the wife being so abused with kicks and blows, reported Winstanley, that "she miscarried of her Child".

Winstanley had another meeting with Platt on Easter Monday, at which the parson again "seemed to consent to many things, and was very moderate". His apparent grievance was that the wood cut by the Diggers to build their houses belonged to him as lord of the manor, and Winstanley understood him to promise that "if the diggers would not cut the wood upon the Common, he would not pull down their houses". So "the diggers resolved for peace sake, to let the wood alone till people did understand their freedom a little more".

The truce did not last. Four days later Platt led another party to the heath. "He came", writes Winstanley in *An Humble Request*, "accompanied with about 50 men, and had hired 4 or 5 of them, to fire down the diggers houses: some that stood by said, do not fire them, the wood will do some good; his answer was, no, no, fire them to the ground, that these Heathens, who know not God, may not build them again; for if you let the wood alone they will build again.

"Thereupon at the Command of this Parson Plat, they set fire to six houses, and burned them down, and burned likewise some of their householdstuffe, and wearing Clothes, throwing their beds, stooles, and householdstuffe, up and down the Common, not pittying the cries of many little Children, and their frightened Mothers, which are Parishioners borne in the Parish. And yet some of these hired men, lives not in the Parish, and some are strangers newly come into the Parish: and so were bewitched by the covetous make-bate Priests, to do this heathenish turkish act.

"The poor diggers being thus suddenly cawst out of their houses by fire, both they, their wives and Children were forced to lie upon the open Common all night: yet the rage of Parson Plat and his Company rested not here, but in the night time, some of them came again upon the Commons, while the diggers were quiet, and some of them in bed, and said, we have Authority from our Master, that is Mr. Plat, to kill you, and burn the rest of your goods, if you will not be gone: thereupon Sir Anthony Vincent['s] Servant, called Davy, struck at one, and cut some of their Chaires and other Goods to peeces, frightening the women and Children again...

"Nay farther, if this satisfies not Mr Plat, but he & Tho: Sutton, of Cobham, have hired three men, to attend both night and day, to beat the Diggers, and to pull down their tents or houses, if they make any more; and if they make Caves in the earth, they threaten to murther them there, so that they will not suffer the poor Diggers to live, neither above nor below ground: if they beg, they whip them by their Law for vagrants, if they steal they hang them; and if they set themselves to plant the Common for a livelihood, that they may neither beg nor steale, and whereby England is inriched, yet will they not suffer them to do this neither."

Some of the Diggers had boldly asked Platt's men why they acted as they did. "They answered, because you do not know God, nor will come to Church. Surely if the God of these men, by their going to Church, teach both their preacher and they, to do such cruel deedes; we will neither come to Church, nor serve their God. Mr. Plat in his Sermons can say, *live in peace with all men, and love your Enemies*: therefore if the Diggers were enemies, he ought to love them in action; but it is a true badge of an hypocrite, to say, and not to do."

Winstanley concludes with what would prove to be the last words he would write about the project to which he had given all his faith, hope, energies, talents and human compassion:

"And now they cry out the Diggers are routed, and they rang bells for joy; but stay Gentlemen, your selves are routed, and you have lost your Crown, and the poor Diggers have won the Crown of glory.

"For first you have not routed them by Law, for you durst not suffer the Diggers to plead their own cause, so that it never came to any tryal and you have no Law to warrant your Lordly power in beating of the Diggers, but the will of Kingly sword-power, which is self-will, and Club-law.

"Secondly, You have not routed the Diggers by dispute; for your impatient, covetous, and proud swelling heart, would not suffer you to plead rationally with them.

"Neither thirdly, have you routed them by Scripture; but the Diggers have routed you by your own Law; by reason, by Scriptures, and patient suffering all your abuses; and now your name shall rot, and your own power shall destroy you...

"They say they have routed the Diggers. But they are mistaken, for the Diggers keep the field of patience, quietness, joy and sweet rest in their hearts, and are filled with love to their enemies; but the Gentlemen are so impatient, they cannot rest for fretting, jearing, rayling, and gnashing their tongues with vexation...

"This work of digging, being freedom, or the appearance of Christ in the earth, hath tried the Priests and professors to the uttermost, and hath ripped up the bottom of their Religion, and proves it meere witchcraft, and cosonage [cozenage: deception]; for self love and covetousnesse is their God, or ruling power. They have chosen the sword, and they refuse love; when the Lamb turns into the Lion, they will remember what they have done, and mourne.

"And thus I have faithfully declared all the business, and though the power of their covetousnesse, self-loving flesh, hath for the present trod our weak flesh down; yet the strength of our inward man, hath overcome them; and is the Lord God Almighty, above that power that rules in them.

"We have declared our Testimony, and now let freedom and bondage strive who shall rule in Mankind: the weapons of the Sonnes of bondage being carnall, as fire, club, and sword; the weapons of the Sonnes of freedom being spiritual, as love, patience, and righteousnesse. Finis."

The other Digger colonies did not long survive the breaking of the mother settlement. The Iver community produced a defiant *Declaration* in May[1], but the digging was done. Winstanley himself, however, was not allowed to put it behind him. He and fourteen others were indicted at the Surrey Assizes for disorderly and unlawful assembly, charges apparently relating to the original dig at George's Hill. Since the records of the proceedings seem not to have survived, we do not know the outcome, but Sabine conjectures that Winstanley may have served a term in jail. Whether or not that was so, the inspiration of the True Levellers was now consigned to the wilderness, deprived of his community and his dream, finally forsaken, it seemed, by a Christ, a spirit of universal love, a spirit of reason, on whose imminent appearance all his hopes and plans had rested.

XI
Mission to the churches

What was Winstanley to do now? He and his comrades had endured a year of extraordinary hardship, violence and abuse in pursuit of a dream. They had been buoyed up through all their tribulations by a religious certainty that theirs was the way of the future, that a reason and justice innate in the cosmos guaranteed the triumph of community over property and their victory over the Beast. Now the dream was shattered, the work undone, the promise unfulfilled. Community had forced a show-down, and property had won. Where did that leave Winstanley and the Diggers?

It certainly removed them from centre stage - if, indeed, they could ever be said to have occupied so prominent a position. The English republic was itself little more than a year old and was still struggling on several fronts, now seeing off the Leveller challenge on the left, now royalist plotters on the right, not to mention the threats posed by a hostile Scotland and Ireland. True Leveller communism was probably never more than an irritation to the new men making their new way in a new government, a troublesome rash on the backside rather than a life-threatening cancer at the heart of the body-politic. It had forced its way onto the political agenda, had become for a time the tittle-tattle talk of the town. But by the end of April 1650 the centre-stage was occupied by other players as the drama of the English republic moved on to a new act with new scenes.

Despite the resourceful researches of recent historians, we still have a broken and incomplete picture of Winstanley's life after the collapse of his communist experiment. We do not know whether or not he went to jail in 1650 or 1651. We know even less of his life after 1652, and the brief snapshots available provide information which is often baffling and apparently inconsistent. But we do know that Winstanley published two more major works, including his most considered and coherent argument for a communist republic, *The Law of Freedom* in 1652. Before that, there was *Fire in the Bush*.

Fire has long been a puzzle to Winstanley scholars. The only known edition is dated 1650 on the title page, but the style and language seem to belong to his pre-Digger period. On the other hand, unlike the 1648 pamphlets it is explicitly communist in its theology. The striking fact that it makes no mention whatever of the Digging communities, while preaching communal occupation and cultivation of land, suggested to Sabine that it was written either in February and March 1649, in the interval between the "trance" and the beginning of work at George's Hill, or in 1650 after the destruction of the communes. Later scholars have championed one date or the other. It is, of course, perfectly possible - and seems to me likely - that Winstanley began *Fire* early in 1649, dropped it when he felt called to act communism rather than write about it in April, then picked it up and dusted it off for publication a year later when continuing action was no longer possible. Certainly the pamphlet has an unfinished feel about it. Indeed, although 13 chapters are listed at the head, only eight are included in the one known edition. Perhaps Winstanley rushed it out to earn a few shillings at a time when he was left with no other means to support himself and his longsuffering wife.

It is, nevertheless, or was intended to be, an ambitious work. Winstanley addresses it to "All the severall societies of people, called churches, in the Presbyterian, Independent, or any other forme of profession, in the service of God", and it has no less a purpose than to persuade the churches that the God they are serving is the devil, who will only be banished when property has given way to community. In an opening address, Winstanley makes the familiar claim that what he has to say is "a free gift from the Father himselfe; And I received it not from men". He says that he held back for a fortnight before obeying "a voyce... in my very heart and mouth", heard as he awoke from sleep, telling him "goe send it to the Churches". This sounds like the Winstanley of early 1649.

The divisions among the churches, he says, "are like the inclosures of Land which hedges in some to be heires of Life, and hedges out others; one saying Christ is here with them; Another saying no: but he is here with them". But Christ "who is the universall power of Love is not confined to parties, or private chambers". His "rising up to fill the Earth" will overcome not only the divided inclosures of the warring churches but the inclosures so beloved of the gentry. "So long as the Earth is intangled, and appropiated into particular hands, and kept there by the power of the sword: as it is, and your profession holds it up, so long the Creation lies under bondage... But if any of you will truly acknowledge Christ, now in the end of your dayes, come joyne hands and hearts together, and set the Earth free; nothing now stands in the way of Englishmen, but inward covetousnesse; Be not like the Rats and Mice, that drawes the treasures of the Earth into your holes to looke upon, whil'st your fellow-members, to whom it belongs as well as to you by the Law of Creation, doe starve for want...

"When you know the Sonne within, as you can talke much of him without, then the Sonne will set you free; and truly he is comming on a maine, to breake downe all your pinfoulds, and to lay all open to the Common."

In the main body of the pamphlet, Winstanley returns to a highly-elaborated and often strikingly original interpretation of scripture's allegories. He re-interprets the Garden of Eden, the Tree of Knowledge of Good and Evil, the Tree of Life, the Serpent, the Soul of man, the Curse and the Blessing. Again, this is very much the stuff of the earlier pamphlets. But where, in 1648, he had not been specific about the form which his republic of heaven would take, here he links "Buying and Selling" with the clergy and lawyers as the "three Beasts" to be overthrown. Christ rising in sons and daughters, "this power of universall love", will "destroy all propriety, and all trading, and bring everything into confusion". The Fall began with selfishness, by which the "elder brother... set about, to inclose parcells of the Earth into severall divisions, and calls those inclosures proper or peculiar to himselfe". Then "mankinde began to buy and sell these inclosures... which the creating spirit of righteousnesse gave them no command to doe; for by reason of this bargaining, the younger, or weaker brother is more forcibly shut out of the Earth, and so here is a foundation laid, to steale the Earth by craft, and to murder one another by the sword... And they that enjoy the land, they or their fathers got it by the Sword, and they kept possession by the Sword... and the whole Earth is filled with this devouring self-righteousnes... This is the battell, that is fought between the two powers, which is propriety on the one hand, called the Devill, or covetousnesse, or community on the other hand, called Christ, or universall Love."

The two "greatest sinnes in the world" are, first, "for a man to lock up the treasuries of the Earth in Chests and houses; and suffer it to rust or moulder, while others starve for want to whom it belongs, and it belongs to all"; and second, "for any man... first to take the Earth by the power of the murdering sword from others; and then by the Lawes of their owne making, doe hang, or put to death any who takes the fruits of the Earth to supply his necessities".

Fire in the Bush seems incomplete, not only because of its missing chapters, but because it is unsure how the Blessing will replace the Curse. This uncertainty fits both pre-digging and post-digging possible dates of composition. Between March 1649 and April 1650 Winstanley was confident that he had a strategy for ushering in the republic of heaven.

Before this period, he was content to leave it all to "Christ rising in sons and daughters"; afterwards, he had only a strategy that had not worked. When he was writing *Fire*, it seems that he had no doubt that the universal power of love, communism or community, would come, but he wasn't clear how or when, or by what agency. The one thing that was quite clear to Winstanley was that the agency was not the republican government, nor the Army, nor the churches. He is contemptuous of all three:

"You oppressing powers of the world, who think God has blessed you, because you sit downe in that Chaire of Government, out of which the former Tyrants are gone: Doe you remember this? your overturning, overturning, overturning, is come on to you, as well as to your fellow break-promises, that are gone before; You that pretend to be saviours of the people, and to seeke the peace of the whole Nation; and yet serve your selves upon the peoples ruines, not regarding the crie of the poore, surely you must have your overturnings too... That Government that gives liberty to the Gentry to have all the Earth, and shuts out the poore Commoners from enjoying any part: ruling by the tyrannicall Law of Conquest over brethren; this is the Government of imaginarie, selfe-seeking Antichrist."

The Army, Cromwell's godly troopers, also served Antichrist. "Therefore you Souldiers... you need not fear that the Levellers will conquer you by the sword; I do not mean the fighting Levellers, for they be your selves; but I mean Christ levelling; who fights against you, by the sword of Love, patience and truth; for whoever takes the Iron sword to fight against you, are your owne sonnes, that fights against you; for Christ came not to destroy, but to save; But Antichrist, whose power you are, came not to save, but to destroy."

As for the clergy (to whom the pamphlet is, after all, addressed), they serve the god of this world, the very devil. As the gentry have shut out the poor from their inclosures, so the university-educated "professors" have "engrosse[d] other mens experimental spirituall teachings to themselves", forgetting that the scriptures were "written by the experimentall hand of Shepherds, Husbandmen, Fishermen, and such inferiour men of the world". "These professors will still confine Christ to a private chamber, and to particular bodies, and restraine him, who is the universall power of Love and peace. They owne him in words, but they denie him in power; they worship God at a distance, not knowing where he is, nor what they worship; And they call this blasphemie, to say Christ is in you." They too shall be overturned, overturned.

If the Winstanley of *Fire in the Bush* places his hopes on any human agency it is the poor. "If you would finde true Majestie indeed, goe among the poore despised ones of the Earth; for there Christ dwells, and there you shall see Light and Love shine in Majestie indeed, rising up to unite the Creation indeed, into the unitie of spirit, and band of peace; the blessing of the Lord is amongst the poore, and the covetous, scoffing, covenant-breaking, thieves and murderers, that croud themselves under the name of Magistracie, shall be sent emptie away."

Nigel Smith has argued[1] that *Fire* was designed to extend the appeal of communism beyond mere digging, in an attempt to reach those various kinds of religious radical who were disillusioned with the Commonwealth and would shortly gravitate towards Quakerism. But the pamphlet does not seem to me to possess such clarity of purpose, and I suggest it should be seen as something of a mongrel work, perhaps written at different periods and reworked in haste before despatch to the printer.

Winstanley's most pressing need was for money. While he may have continued herding other men's cows during the George's Hill occupation, it is likely that this source of income was no longer available to him by the time the Cobham heath community was dismantled. He needed a job, and found one in an unlikely place, as hired hand to a minor aristocrat. During the Diggers' fund-raising campaign in April, his emissaries had passed through Hertfordshire and may have won the sympathy of Lady Eleanor Davies of Pirton, an eccentric poet and "cunning woman" who had published verse predicting the overthrow of Charles I and had been confined to Bedlam for her pains. In a further bizarre twist, Lady Eleanor was later to marry Sir Archibald Douglas, an illegitimate brother of the king she had dethroned in her poetry. But in the late summer or autumn of 1650 she took Winstanley and perhaps a few other former Diggers into her employment on the Pirton estate.

That the True Leveller who had written so passionately only a few months earlier that "buying and selling", including the buying and selling of labour, belonged to man's fallen state should hire himself as a labourer on a gentlewoman's private estate comes as something of a surprise. It raised eyebrows at the time, and has done so on the Winstanley circuit since. Winstanley himself insisted, in a letter to Lady Eleanor in December 1650, that "I came not under your roofe to earne money like a slave. It is the convertion of your spirit to true Nobilitie, which is faln in the earth, not the weight of your purse that I looke after"[2]. Perhaps he did hope to convert a sympathiser into a follower, maybe even to restart his experiment at Pirton under her matronage. But it is clear that he accepted - or at least expected - some kind of financial reimbursement, if not "wages", and indeed complained when what he believed was his due was not forthcoming. The letter just quoted is part of a bitter complaint that Lady Eleanor had failed to pay up. Winstanley appears to have been owed as much as £20, a substantial sum which suggests that several former Diggers may have been on the payroll, with Winstanley responsible for passing on their share of earnings.

It is not clear what work he was doing for Lady Eleanor. A possible clue is provided in a pamphlet by the erstwhile Ranter Lawrence Clarkson, *The Lost Sheep Found*, published ten years later in 1660. Clarkson referred back to the digging experiments and attacked Winstanley's "self-love and vain-glory", suggesting that his object was "by digging to have gained people to him, by which his name might become great among the poor commonalty of the nation" [3]. In what has been taken by most scholars to be a specific reference to the Pirton episode, Clarkson sneers at Winstanley's "most shameful retreat from Georges-Hill... to become a real Tithe-gatherer of propriety". Does this mean that the man who had written, preached and acted so vociferously against tithes as the means of maintaining a corrupt clergy and greedy lay impropriators was actually prepared, albeit as a temporary expedient, to act as Lady Eleanor's tithe collector? Or was Clarkson speaking in riddles?

He and Winstanley, both Lancastrians - Clarkson came from Preston - had certainly clashed earlier. As we have seen, Clarkson may well have visited Cobham Heath with the Ranters who so disrupted the community, and probably took Winstanley's February 1650 anti-Ranter pamphlet *A Vindication* as a personal attack. *Fire in the Bush* had also included what seems to have been a direct attack on Clarkson's doctrine of the "single eye": the idea that light and darkness, good and evil, are to be seen as one. (Christopher Hill points out that Clarkson's *A Single Eye* wasn't published till October 1650, probably some months after *Fire*, but he adds that Clarkson had almost certainly been preaching on the same theme for some time[4]). So Clarkson was no neutral observer. But it is hard to blame Winstanley for hiring himself out - what alternative was there? - and even if the work he engaged to do was repugnant to the principles he had enunciated over the previous two or three years, this hardly discredits either him or them. Engels profited from a factory; William Morris ran a business. Winstanley wasn't the only socialist to earn some much-needed bread within the system he wished to overthrow.

Certainly the Pirton episode, whatever else it was, did not amount to an abandonment by Winstanley of his ideal of the earth as a common treasury of mankind. His final communist manifesto was still to come. Like all his earlier works, it was shaped by the events of the time, the continuing twists and turns of the unfinished revolution. The year 1651 saw twists and turns aplenty.

In 1649 Oliver Cromwell had been chosen chairman of the Council of State, the government of republican England. In June of that year he led a military force to Catholic Ireland, where royalist forces posed a continuing threat to the London regime. By the end of the year much of Ireland was in Cromwell's hands, but a new threat was posed by Presbyterian Scotland, where Charles, son of the beheaded monarch, had been crowned King Charles II. In July 1650, when Fairfax refused to command an invasion of Scotland and retired to private life, it was Cromwell who led the English republican army northwards. He was now Captain-General and Commander in Chief, as well as chairman of the Council of State and Lord Lieutenant of Ireland. By September, after the decisive battle of Dunbar, Cromwell had effectively secured Scotland for the republic. The success of the revolution, it seemed to most contemporary observers, lay in the hands of one man: Oliver Cromwell.

But as Winstanley quarrelled with Lady Eleanor at Pirton at the end of 1650, the republic and the revolution was still one step away from total security. The royalist Scots had been defeated, but a remnant of Charles's army survived at Stirling, and in the spring of 1651, as Cromwell lay ill in London with malaria picked up in the bogs of Ireland, they regrouped and began to pose a renewed threat. Not till Cromwell recovered in June was England's campaign resumed. He sent Lambert across the Forth to attack the Scots from the north, driving them south towards the border. Charles took the ill-fated step of marching his troops into England and towards London, hoping for royalist risings on the way. It was a forlorn hope. When Charles reached Worcester, Cromwell attacked him from two sides. Once again the royalists were defeated, this time decisively. Worcester was Cromwell's "crowning victory", and Cromwell was England's crowning glory, its "chief of men".

Between Dunbar and Worcester there occurred a significant political event which appears to have been the direct occasion of Winstanley's final pamphlet. On January 20 1651 Parliament appointed a Committee to propose such revision of the laws of the land as were necessary to complete the transition from monarchy to republican commonwealth. Winstanley had frequently urged that the Government cease facing both ways, backwards towards kingly power and forwards in paying lip-service to power vested in the people, and complete its unfinished business with a decisive move forwards. The establishment of the Committee encouraged him to hope that just such a move was imminent, especially as the radical Hugh Peters, a member of the Committee, had argued that the old laws should be replaced by new ones derived from the Word of God. Winstanley's view of the "Word of God" wasn't exactly the same as that of Peters, but he acknowledged that "there are good rules in the Scripture". What mattered was that the law reforms which he and the radicals had called for since the dethronement of the king seemed suddenly to have reached the political agenda. Winstanley claimed that he had contemplated putting forward his own reform platform two years earlier. Now he was "stirred up to give it a resurrection, and to pick together as many of my scattered papers as I could finde". As Cromwell climbed to greater triumphs, culminating in Worcester, Winstanley conceived the idea of putting his platform direct to the man on whom the success or failure of the revolution rested. Over the previous three years he had addressed in turn his fellow Lancastrians, the City of London, the Army, his fellow radicals and the churches. It was time now to speak truth to the highest power in the land. And it was to prove his last shot.

XII
If not Christ, Cromwell

We read and evaluate *The Law of Freedom* as Winstanley's last work, the culmination of his four-year crusade to make the earth a common treasury. It is unlikely that Winstanley himself had any sense that this might be his last shot. He acknowledges that the platform he is putting forward is "like a peece of Timber rough hewd", and although he invites Cromwell and his "learned Citizens" to "frame a handsome building out of it", we may suppose that Winstanley hoped to be involved for many years to come in the making of the new society, if not directly, then as a pamphleteer and prophet. But because we know these were his last published words, we are tempted to privilege them above earlier work that seems less mature simply because it is earlier. So *The Law of Freedom* has been commonly viewed as the culmination of a process by which Winstanley moved from mystical theology to secular politics, and thus from an immature pre-modern mode to a mature modernity. That is certainly not how he would have seen it. He would have insisted that all his work, including *The Law of Freedom*, was underpinned by his theology, but that all of it, including his earliest, was wholly secular and political in referring to this world, the real world, in real time and space. For him, the theological and the political were inseparable, as heaven and earth were one, and "Christ" and Reason one.

The Law of Freedom is in three parts: an open letter "To His Excellency Oliver Cromwel, General of the Commonwealths Army in England, Scotland and Ireland"; an address "To the Friendly and Unbyassed Reader"; and the six chapters comprising Winstanley's "Platform", subtitled "True Magistracy Restored". Winstanley starts by telling Cromwell that God has honoured him above all men since Moses, whose casting out of "Oppressing *Pharaoh*" was the model for Cromwell's casting out of "*Norman* Power". But Moses had finished the job. Cromwell's task remained to be completed. "That which is yet wanting on your part to be done, is this, To see the Oppressors power to be cast out with his person; and to see that the free possession of the Land and Liberties be put into the hands of the oppressed Commoners of England. For the Crown of Honor cannot be yours, neither can those Victories be called Victories on your part, till the Land and Freedoms won be possessed by them who adventured person and purse for them." Cromwell must not suppose that he alone had deposed royal power, nor the Army officers. The republic had been made "by the hand and assistance of the Commoners, whereof some came in person, and adventured their lives with you; others stayd at home, and planted the Earth, and payd Taxes and Freequarter to maintain you that went to war". It was plain "Equity, That all the Commoners who assisted you, should be set free from the Conquerors power with you".

With the power in his hands, Cromwell "must do one of these two things:...either set the Land free to the oppressed Commoners... or... onely remove the Conquerors Power out of the Kings hand into other mens, maintaining the old Laws still". "You have the eyes of the People all the Land over, nay I think I may say all neighboring Nations over, waiting to see what you will do". God was watching too. "The Spirit of the whole Creation (who is God) is about the Reformation of the World, and he will go forward in his work: for if he would not spare Kings, who have sat so long at his right hand, governing the World, neither will he regard you, unless your ways be found more righteous then the Kings." (Notice that Reason has become God again: but Winstanley knew that Cromwell was more disposed to obey God than to listen to Reason).

Cromwell is warned of the "common whisperings... among the people": their complaints that, despite their sufferings in the civil wars, "the Taskmasters multiply over us more than formerly"; the Government's "promises are not performed"; parliamentary elections are not being held; religious nonconformists are "cashiered, imprisoned, crushed, and undone... for Conscience sake"; many of the old royalist parish priests remain in place, "buzzing their subtle principles into the minds of the people"; tithes continue to be exacted; and lawyers occupy "the Conquerors Chair", enforcing the old laws "[as] it was in the Kings days". Cromwell's own soldiers, when asked what they fought for, "answered, they could not tell". Lords of the manor continue to exact fines and heriots, "beating them [their Brethren] off the free use of the Common Land". Freeholders "or the new (more covetous) Gentry, over-stock the Commons with Sheep and Cattle, so that inferior Tenants and poor Laborors can hardly keep a Cow"; and "covetous Norman Toll-Taker[s]" continue to exact market tolls "according to the Kings old burdensom Laws, and contrary to the Liberty of a free Commonwealth". The common speech among the people was, "We have parted with our Estates, we have lost our Friends in the Wars, which we willingly gave up, because Freedom was promised us; and now in the end we have new Task-masters, and our old burdens increased: and though all sorts of people have taken an Engagement to cast out Kingly Power, yet Kingly Power remains in power still in the hands of those who have no more right to the Earth than ourselves".

Winstanley denies that the communist platform he proposes will simply turn the tables and leave priests and landlords as a new impoverished class. "For though you do take away Tythes, and the Power of Lords of Mannors, yet there will be no want to them, for they have the freedome of the Common stock, they may send to the Storehouses for what they want, and live more free then now they do, for now they are in care and vexation by servants, by casualties, by being cheated in buying and selling, and many other incumbrances, but then they will be free from all, for the common Storehouses is every mans riches, not any ones." It was buying and selling which "did bring in, and still doth bring in, discontents and wars... And the Nations of the world will never learn to beat their swords into plowshares, and their spears into pruning hooks, and leave off warring, until this cheating device of buying and selling be cast out among the rubbish of Kingly power". Poverty would be abolished, "for there will be plenty of all Earthly Commodities... There will be no want, for every man may keep as plentiful a house as he will, and never run into debt, for common stock pays for all".

Nobody will be "compelled to practise this Commonwealth Government", says Winstanley, "for the spirits of some will be Enemies at first, though afterwards will prove the most cordial and true friends thereunto". This is the position Winstanley adopted in his first communist work, *The New Law of Righteousnes*, though it is somewhat modified in the "Platform" itself, as we shall see. But Winstanley ends his eloquent letter to the General with a summary of what he desires for the people: "That the Commonwealths Land, which is the ancient Commons and waste Land, and the Lands newly got in, by the Armies Victories, out of the oppressors hands, as Parks, Forests, Chases, and the like, may be set free to all that have lent their assistance, either of person or purse, to obtain it; and to all that are willing to come in to the practice of this Government, and be obedient to the Laws thereof: And for others, who are not willing, let them stay in the way of buying and selling, which is the Law of the Conqueror, till they be willing."

Winstanley himself describes his "Platform" as being in his mind for two years - presumably ever since his "trance". It had been laid aside because of "the disorder of the times", but the appointment of a commission to examine and amend the laws had moved him to take it up again. "Therefore I was stirred up to give it a resurrection, and to pick together as many of my scattered papers as I could finde, and to compile them into this method". He had no power to remove "the confusion and thick darkness", and could only "groan and waite for a restoration...

"And now I have set the candle at your door, for you have power in your hand... to Act for Common Freedome if you will; I have no power."

The address "To the Friendly and Unbyassed Reader" is much more succinct - "a short Compendium of the whole". It presents the chief objective of the Platform as the abolition of buying and selling, regulated by the laws of "a free and peaceable Commonwealth". Winstanley knows that the most common fear of his readers is that "community" will lead to anarchy and sexual licence. So he is at pains to emphasise that "Every Family shall live apart, as now they do; every man shall enjoy his own wife, and every woman her own husband, as now they do; every Trade shall be improved to more excellency than now it is; all children shall be educated, and be trained up in subjection to their parents and elder people more then now they are: The Earth shall be planted, and the fruits reaped, and carried into Store-houses by common assistance of every Family: The riches of the Store-houses shall be the Common Stock to every Family: There shall be no idle person nor Begger in the Land". That the community shall be governed by Law is necessary to curb "offences which may arise from the spirit of unreasonable ignorance... For if any man abuse his neighbor, by provoking words, by striking his person, by offering offence to his neighbors wife or children, or to his house or furniture therein, or to live idle upon other mens labours, there are Laws to punish them sharply, and Officers to see those Laws executed, according to the right Order of Commonwealths Government, for the peace of every family in the land". Where, in his letter to Cromwell, Winstanley had shrewdly reflected growing popular disillusionment with republican government, here he no less shrewdly responds to a mounting fear of chaos and the increasingly-heard pleas for a restoration of law and order.

The first two chapters of the Platform itself continue in this defensive mode, anticipating objections and emphasising that the new Law of Freedom he proposes will prevent abuse of freedom. He proposes not the end of magistracy but "True Magistracy Restored" - a distinct shift from his earlier position, in *A Letter to the Lord Fairfax*, that there would be no need of magistrates or laws once the earth was a common treasury. But Winstanley is as free here with Biblical analogy and precedent as he has been in any of his previous works. When he comes to set out the administrative structures of the new society, they are at first glance little different from those of the old: the traditional family at the base, ruled by the father as head of household, then "the bigger Family, called a Parish", then the "County, Shire or Land", and finally the nation ruled by Parliament. But if the forms are familiar, they are transformed by one crucial factor: consent. No-one may exercise authority unless they are chosen to do so. Even the head of a household, Winstanley argues (not entirely persuasively), is a "Commonwealth Officer" because "the Necessity of the young children choose him by joynt consent, and not otherwise". At parish level - and Winstanley clearly means civil parish or township - it is "the whole body of the Parish" that must "choose two, three, or more, within that circuit, to be their Overseers", and again it is the people who must choose county and shire officers. Here is a blueprint for fully representative democracy at local level, not actually realised until the late nineteenth century. And there is to be a mutual obligation, a social contract, between electors and elected. The officers are to discourage and punish breaches of the peace and the Law of Freedom, but the community is to "assist and protect" them, which Winstanley spells out as implying "The rising up of the people by force of Arms to defend their Laws and Officers against any Invasion, Rebellion, or Resistance, yea to beat down the turbulency of any foolish or self-ended spirit that endeavors to break their common Peace".

Winstanley is well aware of the danger that some Officers might be tempted to "take possession of the Earth into their own hands", and proposes a series of measures to discourage any such familiar lurch towards counter-revolution. First, Officers may serve for only one year, necessitating annual elections. "When publique Officers remain long in place of Judicature, they will degenerate from the bounds of humility, honesty, and tender care of brethren, in regard the heart of man is so subject to be overspred with the clouds of covetousness, pride, and vain-glory: for though at the first entrance into places of Rule they be of publique spirits, seeking the Freedom of others as their own; yet continuing long in such a place, where honors and greatness is coming in, they become selfish, seeking themselves, and not common Freedom... And have we not experience in these days, that some Officers of the Commonwealth are grown so mossy for want of removing, that they will hardly speak to an old acquaintance, if he be an inferior man, though they were familiar before these Wars began?" One-year terms would serve to remind Officers that "others are coming after who will look into their ways", which will be an encouragement to act justly. Annual elections will ensure that "whereas many have their portions to obey, so many may have their turns to rule", which will encourage all to "advance Righteousness and good Manners". In this way, "The Commonwealth... will be furnished with able and experienced men, fit to govern, which will mightily advance the Honor and Peace of our Land, occasion the more watchful care in the Education of children, and in time will make our Commonwealth of England the Lilly among the Nations of the Earth".

Secondly, counter-revolution is to be deterred by judicious regulation of both those entitled to vote and those qualified to stand for office. Those who supported the royalist armies, either by fighting or lending money, would be disqualified from both voting and standing. But they should not be reduced to the status of servants, "for they are our brethren, and what they did, no doubt, they did in conscionable zeal, though in ignorance". They are excluded on the ground that "these cannot be friends to common Freedom". Also excluded are Cromwell's new class of land speculators, "All those who have been so hasty to buy and sell the Commonwealths Land... These are the men that take away other mens Rights from them, and they are Members of the covetous generation of Self-seekers, therefore unfit to be chosen Officers, or to choose". Finally, excluded from standing but not from voting are "All uncivil livers, as drunkards, quarrelers, fearful ignorant men, who dare not speak the truth, lest they anger other men; likewise all who are wholly given to pleasure and sports, or men who are full of talk; all these are empty of substance, and cannot be experienced men, therefore not fit to be chosen Officers in a Commonwealth". Winstanley does not say who would decide which of their neighbours was over-preoccupied with sport, or talked too much.

It is worth noting that Winstanley's electorate, despite its exclusion of royalists (for a transitional period), speculators and "uncivil livers", is wider than that proposed by the Levellers, who would have excluded servants and perhaps all hired hands. Winstanley's franchise had no property or class qualification: the head of a labouring household was as entitled to choose his representative as the head of a gentry family - precisely because in the new common-wealth there would be neither bond nor free, neither hired labourer nor landlord. True, like the Levellers, Winstanley does not think to include women among the "choosers", let alone the chosen. But it could be argued that his scheme was flexible in that it gave the vote to the head of household. While this was normatively the "father" of a "family", a single man, or, for that matter, a single woman living alone, might also claim to be head of his or her own household, and thus qualified to vote.

Commonwealth Officers would be chosen from men of good character ("whether they be Members in Church fellowship, or not in Church fellowship, for all are one in Christ"), particularly those who had "suffered under Kingly Oppression" or "adventured the loss of their Estates and Lives to redeem the Land from Bondage, and have remained constant". In addition, there would be an age qualification. Officers should normally be "above forty years of age [Winstanley was 41 or 42!] for these are most likely to be experienced men", though younger men might be chosen if they were judged to be of service by virtue of exceptional gifts or good character. Candidates would be forbidden to put themselves forward: they must await nomination by the community.

Winstanley then turns to the specific titles and tasks of Officers. Each town, city or parish is to have Peace-makers ("three, four or six... or more, according to the bigness of the place"), Overseers, Soldiers, Task-masters and Executioners. Each county or shire would have a Court or "County Senate" consisting of a Judge and the Peace-makers and Overseers of all the constituent towns and parishes. Finally, the land as a whole would have a Parliament, a "Commonwealths Ministry", a Post-master and an Army.

The Peace-makers (who "may be called Councellors") will "sit in Councel to order the Affairs of the Parish, to prevent troubles, and to preserve Common Peace". They will also act as arbitrators in disputes, "hear[ing] the matter, and... endeavor[ing] to reconcile the parties, and make peace, and so put a stop to the rigor of the Law". They will also oversee the Overseers and junior Officers.

The Overseers are of four types. There are "Overseer[s] to preserve Peace", who act as assistants to the Peace-maker. They have a particular responsibility to prevent abuse of the common store-house. Another group oversee and regulate trades, including husbandry, shepherding, the care of horses, dairy work, and the work of schoolmasters, postmasters and ministers (a particularly interesting category to be considered later). A third group oversee the production and distribution of goods, "to see particular Tradesmen bring in their Works to Storehouses and Shops, and to see the Waiters in Storehouses do their duty". Lastly, "all ancient men, above sixty years of age, are general Overseers" or Elders, with a duty to be "generall assistances and encouragers of all Officers... That many eyes being watchfull, the Laws may be obeyed, for to preserve Peace".

The Soldier (or Marshal) is to be, in effect, a chief constable, his work being "to fetch in Offenders, and to bring them before either Officer or Courts, and to be a protector to the Officers against all disturbances". He will have "divers Souldiers under him at his command", but will himself be subject to the authority of the council of Officers. The Task-master controls offenders, "those... as are sentenced by the Judge to lose their Freedome". There are apparently no prisons, but offenders are sentenced to community service, and it is the Task-master's job to put them to work. He has firm disciplinary powers which are something of a surprise to those whose image of Winstanley is the mild pacifist. "If they prove desperate, wanton, or idle, and will not quietly submit to the Law, the Task-master is to feed them with short dyet, and to whip them... till such time as their proud hearts do bend to the Law." As for the offender who runs away, "he shal dye by the sentence of the Judge when taken again". The Executioner "shal cut off the head, hang, or shoot to death, or whip" the runaway and all such offenders who have "highly broke the Laws" by murder or rape.

At county level, the Judge presides over the court or Senate. Unlike judges under the old dispensation, he has no power to interpret the law, only to "pronounce" it. Winstanley naively envisaged the new reformed laws as written in clear, unambiguous English, leaving no room for individual interpretation. The Judge will examine both parties "without a Fee'd Lawyer", hear any witnesses, then "pronounce the bare Letter of the Law". The court (Judge, Peace-makers and Overseers, with soldiers in attendance) will sit four times a year or oftener if need be, moving about the county as the assize courts had done.

The proposed Post-masters are not so much forerunners of our modern postmen as an embryonic communications network. Two are to be elected in each parish and their task is to send monthly reports of local happenings to London for recording in a book, copies of which are then distributed back to the localities. Thus, "if any part of the Land be visited with Plague, Famine, Invasion, or Insurrection, or any casualties, the other parts of the Land may have speedy knowledg, and send Relief". This information exchange would also spread knowledge of any "new invention in any Art or Trade, or in the Tillage of the Earth", whereby "When other parts of the Land hear of it, many... will be encouraged to employ their Reason and industry to do the like, that so in time there will not be any Secret in Nature, which now lies hid... but by some or other will be brought to light". The vision is attractive, but one notes that there is no provision (though also no proscription) of a "free press" of the kind which had sprung up during the civil wars.

Not surprisingly, Winstanley devotes considerable space to consideration of the role of the parish "Minister". It is clear that it is no "hireling priest" he has in mind. Each parish is to elect a minister to serve, like other officers, for one year only. On the "one day in seven" which is to be "a Day of Rest from Labor", when the people "may generally meet together to see one anothers faces, and beget or preserve fellowship in friendly love", the Minister is to read out the news collected by the Post-masters, and read the Law of the Commonwealth, both "to strengthen the memory of the Ancients and for the instruction of the young". But, as with the judges, the laws "shall not be expounded... as if a man would put a better meaning [than] the letter itself".

The Minister may however make speeches "of all Arts and Sciences... As in Physick, Chyrurgery [surgery], Astrology, Astronomy, Navigation, Husbandry, and such like. And in these Speeches may be unfolded the nature of all herbs and plants". And religion? The Minister may also speak "of the Nature of Mankind, of his darkness and of his light, of his weakness and of his strength, of his love and of his envy, of his sorrow and of his joy, of his inward and outward bondages, and of his inward and outward freedoms". Not so much a Sunday in church as one at South Place Ethical Society.

It is not only the Minister who may "make Sermons or Speeches": "every one who hath any experience, and is able to speak of any Art or Language, or of the Nature of the Heavens above, or of the Earth below, shall have free liberty to speak when they offer themselves". The Minister, or Reader, is "not to assume all the power to himself, as the proud and ignorant Clergy have done". Every speaker "is required to speak nothing by imagination, but what he hath found out by his own industry and observation in tryal" - a good definition of what Winstanley meant by experience, or experimental knowledge.

For Winstanley, these subjects *are* religion - or the only kind of religion his common-wealth will promote. To speak of the arts, the sciences and the "Nature of Mankind" is "to read the Law of Nature (or God)... By this means, in time men shall attain to the practical knowledge of God truly... To know the secrets of nature, is to know the works of God... And indeed if you would know spiritual things, it is to know how the spirit or power of wisdom and life, causing motion, or growth, dwels within, and governs both the several bodies of the stars and planets in the heavens above; and the several bodies of the earth below; as grass, plants, fishes, beasts, birds, and mankinde; for to reach God beyond the Creation, or to know what he will be to a man after the man is dead, if any otherwise then to scatter him into his Essences of fire, water, earth and air, of which he is compounded, is a knowledge beyond the line, or capacity of man to attain to while he lives in his compounded body. And if a man should go to imagine, what God is beyond the Creation, or what he will be in a spiritual demonstration after a man is dead, he doth as the proverb saith, build castles in the air, or tells us of a world that is beyond the Moon, and beyond the Sun, meerly to blinde the reason of man."

Winstanley knows (from his own early experience of church-religion, perhaps) what damage the doctrines of the clergy can do to sensitive men and women. "Many times when a wise understanding heart is assaulted with this Doctrine of a God, a Devil, a Heaven, and a Hell, Salvation and Damnation after a man is dead, his spirit being not strongly grounded in the knowledge of the Creation, nor in the temper of his own heart, he strives and stretches his brains to find out the depth of that doctrine and cannot attain to it; for inded it is not knowledg, but imagination: and so by poring and puzling himself in it, loses that wisdom he had, and becomes distracted and mad: and if the passion of joy predominate, then he is merry, and sings, and laughs, and is ripe in the expressions of his words, and will speak strange things; but all by imagination. But if the passion of sorrow predominate, then he is heavy and sad, crying out, *He is damned, God hath forsaken him, and he must go to Hell when he dys, he cannot make his calling and election sure*: And in that distemper many times a man doth hang, kil, or drown himself: so that this divining Doctrine which [the clergy] call *spiritual and heavenly things*, torments people always when they are weak, sickly, and under any distemper; therefore it cannot be the Doctrine of Christ the Saviour." It is a remarkable observation of Puritan angst and the emotionally crippling effect of Biblical literalism.

At the apex of the Free Commonwealth is Parliament, made up of two or more men from each locality, again elected for one year only. First among Parliament's duties is wholesale repeal of the old laws, "that all who have been oppressed... may now be set at liberty to plant in Freedom for food and rayment". The "Commonwealths Land" is now defined rather more widely than Winstanley has ever dare define it before, to include not only the commons, heaths, moors and land confiscated from royalists and speculators, but "in particular... all Abby Lands... Crown Lands, Bishops Lands, with all Parks, Forests, Chases". Eight years later, in the final year of the republic, 1659, George Fox would demand the confiscation of these same lands to alleviate poverty (in a pamphlet quietly omitted from his collected works).

Parliament would control the Army, commissioning its leaders in the name of the Commonwealth. Parliament and Army would be mutually dependent, the Army protecting Representatives from those who "would not obey their proceedings", and Parliament legitimating the policing activities of the soldiers. Winstanley seems to have envisaged not a standing national army, except in time of war, but something akin to a policing network made up of the elected soldiers in each locality.

All children, girls as well as boys, were to have a free education, arranged by their local Overseers. Girls would learn music and to read, sew, knit and spin. Boys would be taught the laws of the Commonwealth, arts and languages, "knowledge of the affairs of the world... [so that] they may be the better able to govern themselves like rational men". When they were of age they would learn a trade. Winstanley was perhaps the first to call for the end of selection in education. There was to be no selecting out of "schollars... trained up onely to book learning", for this lead again to the making of "Lords and Masters". All were to follow "such Trades, Arts and Sciences, as their bodies and wits are capable of" till the age of forty, after which "they shall be freed from all labor and work, unless they will themselves". It was from these early-retired over-forties that the Commonwealth's officers and representatives would be elected.

There was, of course, to be no buying and selling. Goods and produce were to be brought to the common store-house and distributed according to need. Every family would have a responsibility to contribute labour to maintain the stores. There would be both general stores and specialist ones: the iron-shops, hat, glove and shoe shops, corn-houses and so on. Winstanley is as ready as ever to underpin his communism with his theology: "Come hither now, all you who chalenge your brethren to deny Christ, as though you were the only men that love Christ, and would be true to him. Here is a trial of your love: can you be as ready to obey the law of liberty which is the command of Christ, as you would have others to obey your Kingly laws of bondage? It may be you will either storme, or go away sorrowful; does not Christ tell you, that if you have food and rayment, you should therewith be content? and in this common freedome, here will be food and rayment, ease and pleasure plentiful, both for you and your brethren; so that none shall beg or starve, or live in the straits of poverty; and this fulfils that righteous law of Christ, *Do as you would be done by*: for that law of Christ can never be performed, till you establish Commonwealths freedome."

The Law of Freedom closes with what amounts to a draft constitution in sixty-two laws, with the punishment - often drastic - for breaking them. Law 3 decrees that any who administer the law for money or reward "shal dye as a Traytor to the Commonwealth". Law 11 says he who strikes his neighbour "shall be struck himself by the Executioner blow for blow, and shall lose eye for eye, tooth for tooth, limb for limb, life for life". Law 17, "against Idleness", would seem to contradict Winstanley's earlier assurances that no-one would be compelled to join the common-wealth: "If any refuse to learn a trade, or refuse to work in seed-time, or harvest, or refuse to be a Waiter in Store-houses, and yet will feed and clothe himself with other mens labors; The Overseers shall first admonish him privately... If he still continues idle, he shall then be whipt, and be let go at liberty for a moneth longer; if still he continue idle, he shall be delivered into the taskmasters hand, who shall set him to work for twelve moneths, or till he submit to right Order". Other laws impose the death penalty for those who "buy and sell the Earth or fruits thereof, unless it be to, or with strangers of another nation, according to the Law of Navigation" (28), and for "he who professes the service of a righteous God by preaching and prayer, and makes a Trade to get the possessions of the Earth" (40). Thus those who continue to practise as priests and paid clergy "shall be put to death for a Witch and a Cheater". It is difficult to reconcile this with Law 6 which promises that "no man shall be troubled for his judgment or practise in the things of his God, so he live quiet in the land". Winstanley plainly struggles to satisfy two hungers, the one for social justice and the other for security, law and order. It should hardly be necessary to remind ourselves that what may seem draconian to our liberal-democratic minds would have looked very different in an age when the sheep-stealer might be hanged and the refuser of hat-honour flogged.

Winstanley himself knew that his Platform was imperfect, "rough hewd", "like a poor man," he tells Cromwell, "that comes cloathed to your door in a torn country garment, who is unacquainted with the learned Citizens unsetled forms and fashions". The General, and the wider public Winstanley is addressing, are invited to "take of[f] the clownish language, for under that you may see beauty".

Winstanley's language is far from clownish. Here is some of the most impassioned and eloquent political prose in English literature. Here too is a utopian concept of great beauty, beaten in fire on the anvil of the Diggers' bitter experience. Of course its weaknesses are evident to us: its ignorance of laws of supply and demand, its innocence in the dynamics of power, its trust that the good must prevail. But *The Law of Freedom* is a towering achievement, with resonances that were to reach far into the future, and with an inexhaustible capacity to keep alive the enabling dream of a fairer, freer, more equitable society.

England did not go communist in the mid-seventeenth century. Why? Why were the Digger colonies so short-lived? Why was the Platform set out in *The Law of Freedom* ignored, not only by the political classes which it threatened to overturn, but by those who shared Winstanley's disillusionment with Cromwell's regime?

The Diggers' failure to attract any mass following, even among the Levellers and religious radicals, would seem to have three obvious causes. First, the power of the pulpit ensured that any course of action recommended by so scandalously unorthodox a theology as Winstanley's would be preached against as the sure road to hell. It was one thing for Parson Platt's parishioners to be aware of their economic grievances, to know that they were being excluded from the benefits of the republic they had fought for, but another to worship Reason, Community and the Levelling Spirit rather than the familiar father-God of their fathers. Winstanley's religion motivated his actions. But religion must have deterred many from joining him.

Along with the prevailing Puritan respectability ran a deep-seated fear and loathing of anything which recalled, or could be made to recall, the atrocities perpetrated in the name of religion on the killing fields of Europe a century earlier, where Anabaptists and Lutherans had slaughtered each other in an orgy of anarchy and lawlessness. The horrors of Anabaptist levelling, of the monster Muntzer, were far from forgotten - or, where memory showed signs of fading, could be swiftly rekindled. The deep terror of communism, of being rendered propertyless and being deprived of the protection and security of property, was as potent in 1640s England as in 1917 Tsarist Russia. That Winstanley's communist society was to be achieved by non-violence and the rising of something reassuringly called Christ was not enough to allay such ingrained fears. In any case, while the poor looked forward to a day when they would no longer be poor, they hoped to cease being poor by acquiring a little property, not by being in the same boat as everyone else.

But the third reason was economic. The earlier part of the seventeenth century had seen a huge encroachment on England's commons, following a judicial decision in 1605 that cottagers had no rights which were not subject to the will of their lords. For the next thirty years country landowners tightened their grip by drainage, deforestation and enclosure. Poor commoners had to fight to retain what they could of their ancient rights, and for much of the time they fought a losing battle. But the collapse of royal authority in the 1640s put a temporary stop to these encroachments, and commoners managed to claw back some of the rights they had lost. In these circumstances, it was not difficult for the Platts and Drakes to represent the Diggers' actions as nothing but a new model of encroachment. Was it not *their* common which was being dug and planted, their heath which was being burned, their firewood which was gathered? The argument was a cynical one in the mouths of a class which had itself walled and ditched the commons wherever it could get away with it, and had notoriously overstocked the remaining unenclosed land with their own sheep and cattle. But as strangers from outside the area joined the dig, it cannot have been difficult to stir up resentments. When Winstanley was distrained against by the Kingston court it was the tenants who rode from town to town shouting "The Diggers are conquered! The Diggers are conquered!"

The collapse of "True Levelling", following as it did hard on the heels of the collapse of the Levellers, marked the turning point of the republican revolution. By the time Winstanley had collected his papers and written them up in his Platform for Cromwell, the forward impetus had been lost. England was already engulfed in a collective scramble for property and power as a new class of place-men seized the confiscated lands of old royalists, Presbyterians who had refused the Engagement, and Catholics. New money was talking, and if power was passing from the countryside to the town, from the land to commerce, it was no less a power based on property than it had ever been. England had made its revolution, but it was an entrepreneurs' revolution, and it was not going to exchange "particular propriety" for a common treasury. When it was eventually forced to choose, in 1659, between a renewed radical enthusiasm which threatened a return to levelling agitation, and the consolidation of property behind a restored monarchy, it voted with its purse.

By 1652, when *The Law of Freedom* was published, popular disappointment and disillusionment had already begun to find a new expression. The Quakers offered a similar republic of heaven, but more internalised, more spiritualised than Winstanley's: a paradise within rather than without, or at least with more emphasis on personal than social transformation. Quakerism was Winstanley *sans* communism. It had all Winstanley's courage and stubbornness, his flair for publicity and for turning persecution to propaganda advantage, his conviction that action was the life of all; and, of course, much of his humanist religious genius. If it did not complete, or attempt to complete, Winstanley's work, it salvaged much from the wreckage.

XIII
Variations on an enigma: Winstanley and the Quakers

After 1652, the few glimpses we have into Winstanley's life present us with a number of puzzles. First, it seems clear that he ceased to preach communism as a political platform, and never again attempted any practical communist experiment. On the contrary, he seems to have adopted a property-owning and commercially driven lifestyle somewhat at odds with his earlier principles. Secondly, this change seems to have been more complex than the standard descent from radicalism via moderation into reaction, with which we are all too familiar, for the post-communist Winstanley first makes a fleeting appearance as a Quaker sympathiser, at a time when the Quakers were becoming the most radical of the Commonwealth's political and religious dissenters, then resurfaces at the Restoration as a country gentleman and, astonishingly, churchwarden, and finally ends his life in the 1670s as a Quaker again. This strange trajectory has baffled Winstanley students and upset the old True Leveller's admirers. It has even prompted some to wonder aloud whether there was perhaps another Gerrard Winstanley busily, if unknowingly, laying false trails for future historians. I propose first to rehearse what is known, then to suggest that there are perhaps fewer contradictions here than appear at first sight - or, at least, fewer surprises.

Fewer, but those which there are do take some explaining. If R J Dalton is right to date Winstanley's involvement in a family law case to the autumn of 1652, the ink was scarcely dry on *The Law of Freedom*'s denunciations of lawyers, magistrates and courts which "whip the People by old Popish weatherbeaten Laws", before its author was participating in the very system he had so eloquently denounced, seemingly repeating the bewildering pattern by which he had hired his labour to Lady Eleanor Davies shortly after denouncing hired labour in *An Humble Request*. It seems that he agreed to participate in a legal appraisement of his recently deceased brother-in-law's estate, to settle a dispute over money owed by the brother-in-law, Giles Hicks, to his (and Winstanley's) father-in-law, William King. Hardly a compromise of shocking proportions, particularly as it involved his own family affairs, but one which adds to the earlier suggestion of a growing flexibility in action which is not apparent in his words.

If 1652 was the year of Winstanley's last publication, it was also the year when the "Children of Light", the Seekers and other small radical groups and "gathered" congregations came together in the Quaker movement. Thus Quakerism achieved take-off just as Winstanley's own brand of radicalism crash-landed. Newly released from his first imprisonment (for blasphemy) towards the end of 1651, the young George Fox and his companions began their agitations in the north of England, culminating in the mass-following they won in the far West Riding of Yorkshire and Westmorland in the spring and early summer of 1652, and in Cumberland a few months later. The new movement repeated and elaborated many of the insights and teachings of late-1640s radicalism as reflected in Winstanley's own early pamphlets and elsewhere: contempt for the state church in its episcopal, presbyterian or Independent forms; fierce opposition to paid ministers, and resort to civil disobedience in refusal to pay the tithes that supported them; reliance on the inward light of conscience (or "Christ") rather than scriptural or church authority; belief in the "second coming" as both imminent and as an indwelling of believers rather than a physical reappearance in the clouds; and, not least, the conviction that the time had come when the mighty would be put down from their seats, the rich sent empty away, and a republic of heaven (though the phrase is mine, not theirs) would be established on earth, in England, in place of the old corruption of kings, lords and priests.

In the summer of 1652, having won over Judge Thomas Fell's wife Margaret to his cause (and perhaps already to his heart), Fox effectively turned her home at Swarthmoor, near Ulverston, into his missionary campaign headquarters. At first the new movement was largely confined to the north, but by 1654 the leadership, which included Fox and James Nayler, decided to carry their offensive southwards. Francis Howgill, a Seeker pastor till "convinced" by Fox in 1652, and Edward Burrough, a 21-year-old republican militant who joined at the same time, were sent to London in June 1654 "to maintain the war", where they created an immediate stir. Howgill managed to get an audience with Cromwell himself, who disappointed his guest by "crying up the priests" (though Cromwell was probably criticising the notorious Quaker practice of heckling sermons in church, which he considered profoundly intolerant). Anthony Pearson also met Cromwell in July, telling him, in words which might have been borrowed from *The New Law of Righteousnes*, that "Now was the Lord coming to establish His own law, and to set up righteousnes in the earth, and to throw down all oppressors". Howgill and Burrough sent regular despatches to Swarthmoor Hall, often addressed to Margaret Fell who evidently assumed the role of campaign co-ordinator. And it is one such despatch that appears to connect Winstanley to Friends.

In a letter to Margaret Fell, undated but apparently sent in August of that year, Burrough wrote: "Wilstandley sayes he beleeves we are sent to perfect that worke which fell in their handes hee hath bene with us". It is the only apparent reference to Winstanley so far found (by historian Barry Reay) in the archives of early Quakerism. What, then, may we infer from this insubstantial snippet?

Burrough obviously expects Margaret Fell to know who "Wilstandley" is, since there is no explanation or introduction: not "a certain Wilstandley", just "Wilstandley". He also expects her to know what he means by "the work" associated with his new aquaintance. There can be no reasonable doubt that, as Barry Reay believed and Christopher Hill accepted, "Wilstandley", if somewhat mutilated by an idiosyncratic spelling, is our man. Moreover, the statement "He hath been with us", though it could mean no more than that he had passed the time of day with Burrough and Howgill, seems more likely to imply that Winstanley had attended at least one Quaker meeting in London, since meetings were by then established at Simon Dring's house in Watling Street, Robert Dring's in Moorfields, and, as the movement grew, the Bull and Mouth at Aldersgate, which was said to have had standing-room for a thousand.

The intelligence that Winstanley believed the Quakers were or might be the successors of his own scattered movement, sent to "perfect the work" which fell (or had fallen apart?) in his hands, is particularly intriguing. The Quaker leaders in London, and their new enthusiastic followers, were being bitterly attacked as Levellers, the old revolutionaries in a new guise. It would not be surprising if Gerrard Winstanley had come to the meetings to find out just how much of his own radicalism the strangers from the north - his own north - shared and propagated. Indeed, it would be more surprising if he had kept away.

But we know of only this one early Quaker reference to Winstanley. It seems he did not stay with them, and we shall look more closely at the possible reasons for this later. We next hear of him in somewhat different circumstances. Professor James Alsop[1] has shown that in or around 1657 Winstanley's father-in-law, William King of Cobham, made over his property in the manor of Ham in Cobham to his daughter Susan and her husband Gerrard. Although profits on the estate would continue to go to King till his death (which occurred in 1666), Winstanley had the use of it, which was seemingly enough to confer on him the courtesy title of gentleman. By 1659 the Cobham parish registers are recording the appointment of "Mr Winstanly" as a waywarden, in 1660 "Mr Gerrard Winstanley" as an overseer, and by 1668 "Mr Winstanly" as one of the two churchwardens. The Surrey Quarter Sessions order book for the Michaelmas Sessions, 1671 and 1672, further record Winstanley's appointment as one of the two Chief Constables of Elmbridge Hundred[2]. How, indeed, had the humble been exalted! However, the suit he brought in 1660 against the executors of Richard Alsworth, requiring them to produce account books dating back to his time as a merchant taylor in the 1640s, suggests that the nouveau-bourgeois ex-Digger may not have been all that nouveau-riche. He was being sued by the executors for debts totalling £434, much if not all of which he claimed to have repaid long since (specifying among other payments one of £42 plus a piece of blue cloth worth £9, to redeem a loan of £50). The details are confusing, not least since we do not know whether Winstanley contested the debt because he was unable to pay or because he considered it fraudulent. The court's decision is unknown. But that Winstanley had been accepted in the Cobham community as a respectable "Mr" by the time Charles II assumed the burden of reimposing the kingly Norman yoke seems clear enough.

In 1664 Gerrard's wife Susan died. This complicated affairs, as it caused William King to make a new will, revoking his legacy to Susan and Gerrard and leaving his estate to Susan's sister Sarah. Later that year, and deprived now of his gentlemanly status as suddenly as it had fallen on him, Gerrard married again. His wife was Elizabeth Stanley and the Cobham parish registers record the baptism of each of their three children, Gerrard (or Jeremiah) in November 1665, Elizabeth in January 1667 and Clement in October 1669. But after this period of apparent respectability and conformity, stretching from Winstanley's appearance as a waywarden in 1659 to his second appointment as a chief constable in 1672, something seems to have happened to re-ignite the old radical fires. When he died in January1676, his burial at Long Acre is recorded not in the church registers but in those of the Quakers' Westminster Monthly Meeting, where he is described as a corn chandler of Giles in the Field. (His age is given as "about 62" but he was in fact 66).

It has been suggested that Winstanley was not himself a Quaker but that his widow gave him a Quaker funeral in honour of his radical past. This is most unlikely. Quakers did not bury non-Quakers and record them in their registers. The Gerrard Winstanley who died in 1676 and was buried in a Quaker burial ground had evidently thrown in his lot with Friends: that is the inescapable conclusion to be drawn from his inclusion in registers which recorded the births, marriages and deaths only of recognised and acknowledged adherents to the movement. When his widow remarried in 1681, her husband was certainly a Quaker, Giles Tuchbury, cooper, of Giles in the Field, and their marriage took place at the great Quaker meetinghouse at the Bull and Mouth. When, tragically, Winstanley's two sons died young, Gerrard junior in 1683 and Clement in 1684, their burials too were recorded in the Quaker registers[3]. There can no longer be any serious doubt about Winstanley's late reconnection with something of his radical past. As Christopher Hill has commented, "Where else could he go after it became clear that Christ was not going to rise in Charles II's England?" But why did it take him so long, and what sense can we make of his circuitous route?

There is a point which is often forgotten when these apparently enigmatic changes in Winstanley's loyalties are debated, but which is as crucial as it should be obvious. Yes, Winstanley's position changes: it is unstable. But *everything* was changing all around him. Everything was unstable. Aided by a few centuries of hindsight, we tend to oversimplify this bewildering flux by a straight division into 1640s (civil war), 1650s (republic) and 1660s (restored monarchy). But this crude historical trinitarianism hides much more complex processes. Just as the years (or sometimes merely months) of the Rump, the Barebones, the Oliver-Protectorate, the rule-of-the-major-generals and the Richard-Protectorate represented massive u-turns and overturnings in the 1650s, so the first two years of Charles II's rule, which saw a restrained toleration of dissent, were an epoch away from the later sixties and seventies, characterised by the brutal suppression of religious and political dissent under the Clarendon Code, and these in turn were u-turned as changing State interests ushered in short periods of renewed toleration. Winstanley changed: but the religious and political world he inhabited was changing all around him, and at bewildering speed. It is unrealistic and unimaginative to suppose that he could have stood still while all around him the landscape underwent a series of transformations.

Quaker historians tend to lump "early Quakers" together, as if the Quakerism of 1652 was the same as that of 1659, 1661, 1670 and 1680. It wasn't. In its own first generation, Quakerism had its weaning time, its rebellious childhood, its early maturity and its premature middle-age. It changed. Moreover, there were many different strands of Quakerism wefting their own way through the warp of the movement. There were Friends who denied the historical Jesus and Friends who merely subordinated him to the "Christ within"; Friends who refused to fight, and Friends (certainly hundreds, probably thousands, in the 1650s) in the army and navy; Friends who were intensely political and Friends who thought politics too worldly for their attention; Friends who joined with the Ranters in denying an outward God, and Friends who called on an outward God to smite the Ranters. There were Friends for Fox, and Friends for Nayler; Friends for Elizabeth Hooton and Friends for Martha Simmons; Friends for women's liberation within the movement, and Friends who felt more comfortable leaving spiritual leadership in sound patriarchal hands. Quakerism, for many years, till the clammy hand of conformist Nonconformity and respectability fell upon it, was a simmering cauldron of ideas, notions, visions, adventures and inspirations, mixed, like all human endeavours, with displays of passion, leadership contests, power-plays and dramas tragic and comic. Whatever it was, it was not static. We cannot measure a volatile Winstanley against a fixed Quakerism. They both fluctuated, and in 1654 and the mid 1670s their fluctuations brought them together.

Let us, then, so far depart from our rigid documentary methodology as to imagine Gerrard Winstanley in London in 1654 (visiting the city, or once again living and working there?), making his way to the Bull and Mouth. His digging days are behind him, as is his pamphleteering. Both have come to nothing. Christ has failed to keep the appointment Winstanley had made for him, and has not risen in anyone. The republic of heaven remains but a dream. Cromwell shows no sign of ever having read a word of *The Law of Freedom*, let alone of acting on any of it. Parliaments have come and gone. England is effectively a military dictatorship. The engines of the revolution are grinding into reverse gear: the poor are poorer, as to him that hath is given, and from him that hath not is taken away even that which he hath. The earth a common treasury? Not if the Protector and his "new men" can help it - and they can.

And what say these invaders from the dark corners of the north - north even of Winstanley's Wigan - who are drawing crowds of curious Londoners to their Bull and Mouth meetings? In "being with" Friends, did Winstanley find himself among like-minded friends? He would have been instantly familiar with the language he heard all around him: the language of "inner light", of an "inward Christ", of a law written not on tablets or in books but on the heart, of God infused in all men and women, of the iniquity of hireling priests and "dumb dogs", and the hypocrisy of "steeple-house" worship. Burrough at least was as much a political as a religious radical, and Winstanley would have found him fervent for the maintenance of the republic, the onward march of the revolution. Some Friends, including Fox, were demanding (a year or two later, if not then) the nationalisation of church and gentry estates, the abolition of tithes and the liquidation of the clergy as a class. All this would have been music to Winstanley's ears, if perhaps a somewhat wistful, nostalgic music: they were playing his tune, albeit a tune which belonged to all his yesterdays.

But it would soon have become apparent to him that the music contained some discordant harmonies. First, there was what we would now call the pacifist question. Winstanley, through Digger days and propaganda ways, in deed and in word, had advocated nonviolence. The republic of heaven was to be taken by entreaty and not by the sword: this was to be a Lamb's, not a Dragon's war. Parson Platt and his church-mob of bully-boys had been resisted by pleadings, pamphlets, dialogue, propaganda, sometimes ridicule, but never by force. As Christ rose in human hearts, those hearts would be softened: the landlord would lie down with the landless, the powerful with the powerless, and all without a shot being fired. So Winstanley had believed, at least till 1651. If, in *The Law of Freedom*, he had allowed for some continuation of corporal and capital punishment, and of law enforcement by soldiers, he had never lost his conviction that the new heaven and new earth of which he dreamed would be won by co-operation, not coercion. Perhaps he still believed it, or wanted to believe it, in 1654.

If so, he would not have found his sentiments shared by many at the Bull. Early-fifties Quakers were not pacifists. The "peace testimonies" would come later, in the changed climate of the Restoration, when it became imperative for Friends to publicly disavow all plotting and any resort to arms. What Winstanley was likely to hear at the Bull meeting was criticism of the New Model Army and its commanders, not for their use of carnal weapons but for their failure of revolutionary nerve and lack of godly militancy. George Fox would soon be urging Cromwell to liberate Europe and to march on Rome itself: "Let thy soldiers go forth... that thou may rock nations as a cradle". Margaret Fell described the army as "the Battle-axe in the hand of the Lord". Edward Burrough told Cromwell that the republican cause was "the highest on which men were ever engaged in the field", and that it was God, working through the army, who "overthrew that oppressive power of kings and lords... and bishops, and brought some tyrants and oppressors to just execution". I have shown elsewhere[4] that of the 33 men, excluding priests and JPs, named by Fox in that part of his *Journal* describing his 1652 journey from Pendle to Swarthmoor when Quakerism was born, no fewer than 20 can be shown to hold military rank or have army connections, and I have inferred from this that Fox deliberately and consciously targeted the military elite, where he knew he would expect to find political radicals who might be sympathetic to his religious message. Where, to Winstanley, the army had always been the force that kept the Norman yoke in place, even when Norman power had had its head chopped off, to Fox and early Friends it was the last hope of the revolution, the battle-axe indeed of the Lord. I have called this "the Quaker-military alliance", and while the term perhaps oversimplifies a complex web of confusions and contradictions, I am not persuaded that it is entirely inappropriate.

Secondly, there is the matter of "quaking" itself. It is unlikely that, on entering the Bull, Winstanley found himself in the kind of silent meeting we ourselves are familiar with today. In the great hall at the Bull there was often more than one Quaker meeting going on at the same time, with one spirit-filled "mechanick preacher" praying here, a quaking woman prophesying there, and perhaps a soldier or politician agitating away in the corner, all punctuated by groanings and ecstatic ejaculations. Quaker meetings could be noisy, impassioned affairs. And Quakers were notorious for their outlandish behaviour, which was often seen by their contemporaries as ill-mannered and anti-social - particularly the heckling of ministers in their pulpits, the seemingly exhibitionist practice of "going naked for a sign", and the occasional claims (made by Fox, among others) to miraculous powers. It seems likely that a man like Winstanley, who equated God with Reason, would have found such charismatic behaviour irrational and unattractive. Moreover, his own unhappy experiences with "Ranters", with whom the more exuberant Quakers were often identified, would surely have made him wary of "quaking" in its most unrestrained and inspirited forms.

Thirdly, and most important, there was the property question. The abolition of "particular propriety" and its replacement by a "common treasury" had always been at the heart of Winstanley's gospel, at least till 1652. But he would have found few echoes of this in the babel of voices at the Bull. Quakers were intensely political, parliamentarians and republicans to a man and woman (I defy anyone to produce a single royalist Quaker before the 1660s), but they lacked a coherent political programme, and in so far as they had a programme at all it emphatically did not include the "true levelling" of communism - much as their most suspicious or malicious opponents tried to claim otherwise. Friends were much closer both in programme and in strategy to the "official" Levelling of John Lilburne (who of course became a Quaker in 1656, shortly before his death). Like the Levellers, they agitated for mechanisms by which the poor might be relieved and the hungry fed. Unlike the "True Levellers", they did not - with a very few exceptions - demand that the poor take power themselves, feed themselves, partake themselves in a common treasury. In the language of three centuries later, their economic approach was liberal rather than socialist. It could hardly have been otherwise, given the early predominance of George Fox and his strategy of winning over the decision-makers, who tended to be at least modestly propertied: people like the Fells of Swarthmoor, who had done well out of the war and risen from modest "middling sort" status to influential gentry, well regarded and rewarded by the republican administration whose interests they served because it served their interests. Today's Quakers tend not to notice the paradox that what was undoubtedly one of the most radical and socially "progressive" movements of the mid seventeenth century was run, in its early years, from the country mansion of a wealthy Government official and his cultured wife and family. But it is hard not to conclude that Fox's dependence on the Fells, both on their considerable influence and on the rest and comfort they could provide, may have blunted the cutting edge of the movement's commitment to social, if not religious, equality.

It is quite possible, of course, that Winstanley himself had abandoned communism in disillusionment by 1654, but his remark to Burrough and Howgill about Friends continuing his own work suggests not, unless his own conception of his work had itself been somewhat revised. One wonders what went through Margaret Fell's head when she read the letter from London with its suggestion that the movement to which she was already acting as mother-superior might pick up the mantle of a man whose communist experiments were by no means forgotten, and whose notorious pamphlets were widely read - and, indeed, still selling. Did she show the letter to George? Or, even more intriguingly, to her husband Thomas, whose position as a senior law officer and enforcer of Cromwell's writ in the

North-West obliged him to defend property rights above virtually all else?

These are idle (but hopefully not unintelligent) speculations. What is quite clear, however, is that if Winstanley flirted with the Quaker leadership in 1654, the radicalism he encountered in the new movement was different in several important ways from that of his own past work. On violence, on "reason" and on property, Quaker-levelling and Digger-levelling were at odds. This may explain why the flirtation was apparently short-lived. We have no further references to Winstanley from the Quaker leadership in the fifties and sixties, nor does his name crop up again in any of the Quaker records of those decades. Had he "joined" the movement (which actually had no formal membership, but nevertheless took some care to recognise and record who was owned and who was not), his name, famous for some, infamous for others, would surely have attracted attention both from Friends and foes. It did not, at least not at the time, and we must conclude that Gerrard Winstanley did not become one of the regulars at the Bull and Mouth.

Instead, barely three years later, the benevolence of his father-in-law makes of him a country gentleman in the very parish whose commons he had tried to cultivate "in common" a few years earlier. And only two years later still he is on the ladder which will take him from waywarden to overseer and from churchwarden to chief constable.

It is indeed a startling shift of position, but not one that totally passes understanding. If, as we have surmised, Winstanley found Quakers too closely aligned with the army and too Ranterish in their unseemly behaviour, the disillusionment he experienced in 1651 and 1652 will only have been intensified in 1654. If he had indeed hoped that these spirit-filled men and women from the north, who spoke the language of his pamphlets, would perfect the True Levellers' work, he can only have suffered yet one more disappointment. Perhaps his brief encounter with the Quakers' movers and shakers at the Bull finally persauaded him that he was mistaken: that his great God Reason had failed or forsaken him. What alternative did he have, then, other than to make his peace with mammon, to earn a living for himself and his wife - and to take the opportunity of settling as a country gentleman when it unexpectedly came his way? Who among us can be sure that we would have acted differently in his place? And once that big step was taken, it must have seemed a fairly small one to make his peace with the God of the churches, the God of propriety and Norman law and order. The god Reason had forsaken him: what further allegiance did he owe to a god that had failed, and conspicuously humiliated him?

We need to remember that when Winstanley is first recorded as a parish official in Cobham in 1659, England was still a republic and the bishops' Church was still officially outlawed. The ancient parish system had been retained, but the episcopal system was defunct and the Anglican prayer-book services were illegal. Vicars were not "priests" but "ministers", and many were Puritan Baptists, Independents and Presbyterians who could not possibly know that within a few years they would be ejected from their livings. We do not know the religious-political complexion of Cobham in 1659, but it is easy to see how Winstanley might have persuaded himself that the compromises and u-turns he was making fell well short of going over to the old episcopal enemy. Once made, such compromises are difficult to throw into reverse. When the king, bishops, parish priests and prayer-book services were restored, and the nonconformist ministers kicked out of their livings, Winstanley stayed put. And he stayed put, even when the death of his wife Susan deprived him of his father-in-law's legacy and thus of his landed status. After all, what was there then to encourage him to turn back? But by the mid seventies something had happened to turn the wheel again. As we have seen, in 1671 and 1672 Winstanley was appointed one of the two chief constables for Elmbridge Hundred. Four years later, at the time of his death in 1676, he was owned as a Quaker. What persuaded him at this late stage to abandon his hard-won respectability and revert to something approaching the radicalism of his former years and, surely, truer self?

One suggestion[5] is that Winstanley became sickened by the bitter persecution of nonconformists in general and Quakers in particular after 1662, reviving his old fellow-feeling for those who suffered pain, ruin, imprisonment and sometimes death for their conscientious objection to church and state power. But the evidence can be made to point both ways. The first long period of persecution under the "Clarendon code" lasted from 1662 to 1669, when Winstanley seems to have been so untroubled by it as to have served several terms in parish posts. During the operation of the second Conventicle Act, Marvell's "quintessence of arbitrary malice", which lasted from 1670 to 1672 and was characterised by a concerted attempt to liquidate Quakerism and radical sectarianism, Winstanley performed the office of chief constable for his Hundred, in which capacity he was clearly expected to act as persecutor rather than protector of Friends.

In March 1672 the king issued a Declaration of Indulgence declaring the suspension of the Penal Laws, and in the wake of what was in effect a public confession that the policy of repression and persecution had failed, the Quakers petitioned successfully for the release of their many hundred comrades in jail. But the royal Indulgence lasted barely a year. By March 1673 the Penal Laws were back and the jails started filling again with Friends and other recalcitrants. In February 1675 an Order in Council directed that the laws be executed with still more diligence. It is possible that this last tightening of the screws was the straw which broke the back of Winstanley's complacent conformity.

But there may also have been more personal factors at work. In1664, the same year in which his wife Susan died, Winstanley remarried. His wife, as we have seen, was Elizabeth Stanley and they married conventionally in church. But Elizabeth may already have had Quaker connections, and it is possible that she was instrumental in his eventual convincement. She certainly married a Quaker, in a Quaker marriage ceremony, after Winstanley's death, and brought up Winstanley's children as Quakers. Yet another factor is that the family appears to have moved from Cobham back into London some time between 1672 and 1676. When Winstanley died he was described in the Quaker burial register as a "corn chandler" of (St) Giles in the Field, Bloomsbury. The move would have given Winstanley an opportunity to break with the respectable society of Cobham and again make contact with the thriving radical underground of the city. (Some critics have made much of his work as a buyer and seller of corn, contrasting this with his principled opposition to all buying and selling in *The New Law of Freedom*. But the radicalism Winstanley returned to in the 1670s was not the communist radicalism of 1649-52, because the radicalism of the 1670s could not be the radicalism of the 1650s. Liberal "Levelling" politics was just possible, though fraught with danger to life and livelihood: communist "True Levelling" was no longer on anyone's agenda, and there is again little sense in lamenting that it was no longer on Winstanley's).

Why should Winstanley make common cause in the seventies with the same Quaker movement he had apparently flirted with but dumped in the fifties? Because it was *not* the same Quaker movement. Like the world around it, Quakerism had changed. It had long abandoned the heckling of preachers in their pulpits, the practice of going naked as a sign, and other Ranterish behaviour. The spirit-filled Naylers and Burroughs were dead, the sober respectable Penns and Barclays were in the ascendant. The movement was now pacifist, and its political agenda reformist. It described itself as "the harmless people of God called Quakers". In its opposition to tithes, priests, and religious authority, and in its bold insistence that conscience took precedence over all outward authority, even that of the king himself, it remained far more radical than its self-descriptions suggested, and its culture of resistance helped create the notion of "loyal opposition" which in turn made possible modern democratic pluralist society. This was not quite turning the world upside down, "overturning, overturning, overturning", but it did give the world a vigorous push to tilt it onto its side. And by the last few months of his extraordinary life it was tilting rather than overturning which spoke to Winstanley's condition.

It remains, before we finally consider what the seventeenth-century Winstanley has to say to his twentyfirst-century readers, for us to look briefly at the question often raised by modern scholars: What influence, if any, did Winstanley have on Quakerism? The then Dean of Durham, Thomas Comber, it will be remembered, wrote in his pamphlet *Christianity no Enthusiasm* in 1678, only two years after Winstanley's death, that the Quakers "derived their ideas from the communist writer Gerrard Winstanley", which was why, in Comber's view, "repression of Quakerism was not only a service to God, but a preservation of every man and his property". We have seen that this view hardly accords with the historical facts. If Winstanley and Friends shared a common radical religious base, they soon came to draw different political and economic conclusions from their similar visions of a new heaven and a new earth. But how common was their radical base, how similar their visions, and did Winstanley's work, which immediately preceded the rise of Quakerism, influence Friends at all?

The first modern historians to address the question were the revisionist-Marxist theoretician Eduard Bernstein in *Sozialismus und Demokratie in der grossen Englischen Revolution*, 1895, and G P Gooch in *English Democratic Ideas in the Seventeenth Century*, 1896. Both suggested that Winstanley became a Quaker on the basis of the perceived similarity of his and Fox's writings. Lewis H Berens in *The Digger Movement in the Days of the Commonwealth*, 1906, went a stage further in asserting that Winstanley's pamphlets were the source from which Fox and Friends derived their doctrines. These views were contradicted by David Petegorsky in his *Left-Wing Democracy in the English Civil War: a Study of the Social Philosophy of Gerard Winstanley and the Digger Movement*, 1940, which stated flatly - and correctly, at the time of writing - that "there is no evidence whatever" for any direct contact between Winstanley and Friends. Such similarities as there were, he put down to "the result of the general environment of the period". In this view he followed the great Quaker historian William C Braithwaite who had written in his huge study *The Second Period of Quakerism*, 1919, that Winstanley and Fox "seem to be independent products of the peculiar social and spiritual climate of the age", adding that it was therefore "doubtful if Winstanley ever influenced Fox or associated with Friends". And there, for lack of firmer evidence, the matter lay till a later generation of diggers in the archives (notably Vann, Alsop and Reay) unearthed the records which have established connection, if not direct influence.

The Quaker scholar Richard T Vann made a renewed effort, in the *Journal of Friends Historical Society*, Vol 49 (1959-61), to marshal the arguments for confluence, if not influence. His article, entitled "From Radicalism to Quakerism: Gerrard Winstanley and Friends", notes "the striking similarities" which had "long been remarked": hostility towards the ecclesiastical powers for setting up the teachings of men against those of the spirit; teaching according to books and authorities rather than the indwelling God; the maintenance of ministers by compulsory tithes; and so on. But in the end he feels unable to go any further than Braithwaite in concluding that these common positions were probably arrived at independently, under the influence of "the peculiar social and spiritual climate of the age".

That these positions were indeed the common property of many different radical groups in the 1640s, ranging from several kinds of Baptist through the various Seeker communities and "gathered churches" to the Ranters, has been made clear beyond dispute by Christopher Hill (in *The World Turned Upside Down*) and those who have further sifted the soil he has ploughed. Indeed, many more similarities may now be enumerated: an anti-Calvinist theological universalism; the language of "inner light", "seed" and other shared metaphors; a non-literal or metaphorical interpretation of scripture (understood as a secondary rather than primary authority); an apocalyptic expectation that a New Age was about to dawn; assertion of the rights of women and servants to preach and teach; and such radical egalitarian social "statements" as refusal of "hat honour". All this is in Winstanley's writings from 1648 to 1652, and in Fox's from 1652 on.

Can we really believe that George Fox came to his mature religious convictions without ever reading a word of Winstanley or his contemporaries? Is it likely? As we have noted earlier, Fox was as anxious as Winstanley himself to assert that he knew what he knew not from other men and their writings but direct from the Spirit. They both understood *Jeremiah*

31:33-34 as a prophecy applying particularly to themselves - but we are not obliged to take the same view. Fox tells us in his *Journal* how, in the critical years of the 1640s, he thirsted for spiritual knowledge, looked for it everywhere, tried and tested everything on offer. Are we seriously to suppose that this process of intense spiritual inquiry, so common in these troubled times, particularly among earnest young men and women who felt a divine breath on their necks, did not include reading - and, in particular, the reading of the pamphlets and broadsheets pouring off the radical presses, including Giles Calvert's, where both Winstanley and Friends first appeared in print?

It seems to me that, only if our view of Fox is so clouded by a critically-blind Quaker piety that we feel obliged to adopt his view of things (and of himself) without rational historical appraisal, can we hold to the position that the younger seeker after truth was wholly ignorant of the writings of his remarkable predecessor, whose pamphlets were, for four years - Fox's formative years - the talk of the nation. That Fox did read them, learn from them, and inwardly digest their teachings seems plain beyond reasonable doubt. Fox may even have borrowed elements of Winstanley's literary style, apparent sometimes in the freshness and spontaneity of the *Journal*.

If Fox and his young comrades were directly influenced by Winstanley's writings, they would hardly have made a song and dance about it. They needed to assert their own access to divine inspiration, and *Jeremiah* gave them the authority so to do. In any case, by 1652, when Quakerism was up and running, Winstanley looked to be something of a forlorn failure, the prophet of a god that had already failed, and a god that had few attractions for the kinds of "middling-sort" people, including Cromwell's supporters in the army, whom Friends were most assiduously targeting. So the early Quakers never acknowledged their debt to Gerrard Winstanley - and they seem to have got away with it till the Dean of Durham sought to smear them with Winstanley's communism in 1678. And by that time it was a smear without substance. Friends had already set their faces towards property-owning democracy, and in the next century would play their part in the rise of industrial capitalism.

XIV
Postmodern Winstanley

From our perspective, analysing mid-seventeenth-century events with end-of-twentieth-century and early-twentyfirst-century eyes, we are likely to conclude that the Winstanley of 1649 was tragically, if heroically, mistaken. He was convinced that the age of greed and private property was in its death throes, to be succeeded by the age of true common-wealth. It did not happen that way. It did not happen at all. Winstanley's Devil, selfishness, tightened its grip, and the rising of Christ and Reason was indefinitely postponed. When a form of communism was eventually tried on a national scale two and a half centuries later, and not in the chosen land of England, it quickly became a nightmare version of Winstanley's dream. Now, in the wake of the nightmare's collapse, we are still struggling to find form and substance for a dream we can't stop dreaming.

Jesus of Nazareth had had much the same experience. The kingdom he preached as imminent had failed to arrive. He was put to death, bitterly demanding to know why his God had forsaken him and his cause. And when those who followed him tried to give his dream substance, they produced a grotesque distortion. As generations of disillusioned followers have observed, Jesus promised the kingdom and what we got was the Church.

And yet both dreams - Jesus's and Winstanley's - persist. It seems that we are incorrigible dreamers, inured to continual disappointment and failure, stubbornly attached, in the face of all the evidence of history, reason and human psychology, to an irrational conviction that hope might yet triumph over experience; which is why Winstanley contines to fascinate and inspire us three and a half centuries after his words and actions, when his early-modern world-view has given way, first, through one set of historical and intellectual revolutions, to that of mature modernity, and finally, through still greater convulsions, to the wholly transformed outlook of our own postmodern age.

Winstanley's "failure" was one of both theology and politics. While he did not believe in a personal God, he lived and moved and had his being in "God" conceived as a spirit of reason, righteousness and goodwill infused throughout the universe. Winstanley's impersonal God had a will and purpose, no less than Jesus of Nazareth's personal one. God's will for the natural world, what Winstanley was happy to call "creation", was benign.

Humanity's task (by a reasoned understanding of, and reflection on, its own experience) was to seek out and then live in harmony with this benign purpose which underpinned the universe. What made for harmony, happiness and the fulfilment of God's will was a sense of community and interrelationship so powerful that it overrode private interest. The good society, the common-weal, was built on a foundation of disinterestedness and unselfishness: acts of loving kindness, care for others, sharing, a sense of humanity as one family, the peaceful resolution of disputes, the dispersal of authority, a concern for the liberty of others as well as oneself, and living out the worth-equality of men and women - all of which is summed up by loving one's neighbour as oneself and doing to others as one would be done by. To these one might add, in Winstanley's own case, a conviction that "God's creatures" must be treated with due respect - Rabisher was probably right in thinking him a vegetarian - and that the natural world, as the very clothing of God, was to be husbanded with due veneration. All this Winstanley summed up as community or Reason: a reasonable mode of life for creatures endowed with the capacity to reflect on their experience, their experimental or experiential living, by which reason the selfish passions which led to greed and the will to dominate others could be controlled and subdued. "Reason" for Winstanley was not just the rationality, the ratiocination, that it became in the eighteenth century Age of Reason: it was an order and harmony in human life which reflected an order and harmony built into the cosmos itself: sweet reason.

If the cosmos was indeed ordered and harmonious, and somehow imbued with benign purpose and a will-to-good, faith in such providence and co-operation with its benevolent will and intention was the way to make a better world. So Winstanley believed. Our postmodern age no longer sees things this way. Postmodern western man and woman no longer believes that the cosmos has any demonstrable or discernible purpose, it just *is*: neither benign nor malign, neither moral nor immoral. It is essentially purposeless and value-free: neutral. Or, to put it another way, if it has meaning, purpose and value, it is the meaning, purpose and value that we humans, in the whole package of human experience we call imagination and culture, have chosen to put into it. Indeed, we have come to think of the cosmos itself as a human creation, no less shaped by our culture and language than everything else we think we know and experience. And that is the measure of the shifts of outlook which have taken place, first since the civil wars of three and a half centuries ago and subsequently since World War Two.

We can no longer "believe in" Winstanley's theology in the way he believed in it and trusted to it. Christ will not rise in sons and daughters to some cosmically ordained timetable. There *is* no timetable, and no-one to time or tabulate the blind processes of the cosmos. Destiny died with almighty and everlasting God. We share with Winstanley the view that the Bible books are more mythology and allegory than history, but we do not share his assumption that the Hebrew prophets and the author of *Revelation* had some mystical access to knowledge of future events in one of Europe's off-shore islands some seventeen centuries and more after they were writing, and cleverly encrypted this knowledge till it was time for their prophecies to be fulfilled. We value the Bible differently: as ancient wisdom in story form, as enduring poetry and food for the imagination, as the foundation of our western culture, and therefore of who and what we are: but not as "divine revelation", "Truth", or the word of God, or even of Reason or Christ or community. If we do, we are living in the past.

So postmodern western humankind on the cusp of the twentieth and twentyfirst centuries can research and hope to understand Winstanley's theology, but cannot be expected to share it in ways he would recognise. We have a different set of *logia* for our different conception of *theos*. Our continuingly (and stubbornly) high valuation of Winstanley, therefore, and our refusal to consign him and his work to history's dustbins, must be rooted elsewhere. If it is not his flawed theology which fires us, what is it? Simply his politics?

As we noted in the first chapter, it was the Marxists who rediscovered Winstanley in the nineteenth century, and it is in the many strands of socialism derived from Marx that Winstanley has retained his place of honour. Marxism-Winstanleyism preceded Marxism-Leninism. To the first Marxist scholars, Winstanley was himself a proto-Marxist before his time: one had only to strip away the religious language of his pamphlets - seen then as an embarrassing feature of "primitive" or "utopian" communism" which a secularized "ascent of man" had rendered obsolete - to reveal a prophet of economic determinism and historical necessity. Thus Winstanley came to be studied in Soviet academies when he was long forgotten in Wigan and Cobham. (Early Quakerism was also studied in the Soviet Union in the 1960s and 1970s, till some students showed signs of preferring Quakerism to Soviet-style Marxism, at which point the courses showed a remarkable tendency to wither away). As Soviet communism was revealed as the monstrous destroyer of liberty and hammer of the human spirit which it quickly became when it assumed total power, Winstanley's apparently milder, more idealistic or "spiritual" version seemed to some to offer an alternative peg on which to hang stubborn hopes and illusions. But that too could not last.

The years 1848 to 1917 saw Marxist communism become an idealised secular religion for thousands of intellectuals and hundreds of thousands of working men and women. The years 1917 to 1990 saw this secular religion put into practice across (at its height) one sixth of the world. Then, after a life of less than one and a half centuries, it abruptly collapsed. If God was dead, Marx had followed him to the grave. Nor was it just socialism on the Soviet model which failed to deliver. In the west, the disparate and competing strands of democratic socialism and social democracy (also derived, of course, from Marx) were faltering too. In Britain and Scandinavia, Germany and France, Italy and Spain, parties which had once promised regimes of common ownership found themselves obliged to drop their equivalent Clause Fours as the price of electability and survival. So all the socialisms joined all the other isms in the junk-heap of grand narratives which had served a purpose in modernity, only to prove inadequate for the postmodern age. Postmodernity and socialism are not, of course, incompatible. But what we can no longer believe, what we can no longer pin our lives to, is the idea that any ism has some ultimate and absolute authority, rooted in any kind of superhuman purpose or necessity, metaphysical, physical or historical.

No-one today, I imagine, believes it possible to build Winstanley's republic of heaven by the methods he advocated: digging the commons and relying on Reason to look after the rest. Nor does anyone seriously suggest that his *Law of Freedom* still offers a blueprint for today's political activist and humanitarian idealist. Winstanley's first agent of change - the process he described as "Christ rising" - has been dropped from our political vocabulary (if not necessarily from our poetic and expressive one) and, to that extent, can no longer be an agent of anything except imagination. His second agent, state power, has been tried and has failed so catastrophically that it has left the stormtroopers of private property in sole possession of the field - at least for the time being. The common-wealth will not be dug by spades on commons, nor by shaming the rich to join the poor. It will not be forced by the Dragon of coercion and violence, but nor will it be eased by Winstanley's Lamb of universal love. We live in a different world. Winstanley's project, like that of the early Quakers, was experiential. So too must ours be. And our experience is quite different from his and theirs.

Winstanley's legacy for us and, I believe, for future generations, is the enduring dream of the earth as a common treasury. Not his specific ends, not his particular means, but the dream. And not an idle dream, the dream of sleep and rest to which we retire when the hard work is done, but an *enabling dream*: an inspiration to renewed action.

The dream can still inspire because we *choose* to be inspired. We can act because we *decide* to act. We know there is no guarantee of "success" or "victory", whatever these may turn out to be: no historical inevitability, no blessed assurance that all shall be well and all manner of things shall be well. Indeed, our experience insistently suggests otherwise. But we also feel a divine discontent with what we have and what we are. We may know that the cosmos is a void, de-void of purpose, value, intelligence: but we feel we are programmed to a-void the void, to de-void it of voidness, to fill the vacuum with our own purpose and value. So we raid our imaginations to give life shape and meaning, and we do so through our poetry, our drama, our dance, our music, our painting, our stories, our politics, our science, our philosophy, our religion, our investment in love, fellowship and community. No Dragon can put a stop to all that. It may puff in our faces, but we'll fly our flags against the wind. Which is why we carry on telling ourselves, and we mean it, that we shall not cease from mental fight, nor shall our swords sleep in our hand, till we have built Jerusalem in England's green and pleasant land - or Scotland's, or New Zealand's, or Planet Earth's.

No divine plan or materialistic determinism will make the earth a common treasury. Nor can we place any final confidence in any human plan (and there is no other kind) to build the new heaven and new earth (and the two are one). What we can do, what the Winstanley story can inspire us to do, is *choose* to act as if the earth were indeed a common treasury - because the *as if* becomes the *is*. I am not talking about some mystical, spiritualised millenarianism. I am saying that when we make political decisions to treat the earth as a common responsibility and a common treasure, it begins to become so in fact.

Is not this how our stories work - the stories which both make and reflect our dreams, which in turn make and reflect our values? The vision of men beating swords into ploughshares inspires men to beat swords into ploughshares, and every new visit to the anvil is re-told in hi*story*, which re-telling and re-shaping in turn inspires re-enactment, repeat performance. Our values have no objective existence as fixed entities, somehow separate from the natural or real world, like Plato's Forms or Ideas of the Good and Beautiful, untouched by human hand or ineffably uncontaminated by language. The form they do have is a text-form, in story and history. The values of community and interconnectedness, of generosity and co-operation, of sharing and loving-kindness, of amity and peace-making, born as they are of our uniquely human capacity to empathetically imagine ourselves in others' shoes, are themselves communicated, shared, passed on, in the stories we tell with the express purpose of passing them on. If this is true of our mythologies and fictions (our "Norman yoke" stories, our John Ball traditions as told, for instance, in William Morris's *Dream of John Ball*, and our great store of "kingdom of God" narratives), it is no less true of our histories. Indeed our hi*stories* have one major advantage as value-carriers over our fictional stories: they are open-ended in a way fictional stories can never quite be. A good made-up story has a beginning, a middle and an end. History, as Mary Warnock reminds us in *Imagination and Time*, has only a beginning and a middle. It is "a story with no end. We are in the middle of it; and whatever it cannot tell us, it can tell us something of how we got to be where we are... And because history has no denouement, because it is not yet finished, it is a matter of great importance to enable the next generation of humans to go on with the story as they choose, to understand the story so far, and contribute to the construction of the next chapter".

However we determine to write the next chapter, to continue the story, it cannot be a mere repetition of what has gone before. We may celebrate past attempts to give life to the values of community by, say, holding all things in common (the early Church, very briefly), by digging the commons (Winstanley, very briefly), by nationalising the commanding heights of the economy (post-war Britain, briefly), but our next chapter has to be a new chapter. The values which are driving us may be old as human community but must be new every morning if they are to be sharp enough to make serviceable tools for the reshaping of history. We may still wish to say expressively that Christ will yet rise in sons and daughters, but the text is ours now, not Winstanley's. We know (as Winstanley knew) that the Christ Jesus who was executed at Calvary will never rise in any literal sense, and we also know (as Winstanley did not) that there is no preordained destiny by which we may be certain that Christ as a cosmic spirit of sweet reason will come and make an end of history. But why should we not appropriate the poetry? The Christian believer appropriates the words of her church's liturgy, though they can no longer mean exactly what they meant to those who wrote them. The socialist too has a mythology and a rhetoric to which she clings, for continuity, stability, and inspiration. Winstanley's words are not his "particular propriety": they are ours to use in common, and so long as their poetry retains the power to stimulate the imagination and shape our enabling dreams, for just so long may it stir us to look for new ways of building community.

What can we usefully say about what these new ways might be? Winstanley would no doubt despair (even more than he *did* despair in his own time) if he were to rise from his Long Acre grave and take the short walk into the city of London where he had done business, first as a cloth merchant and later as a corn dealer. The concentration of private capital, here in a single pair of hands, there in a corporation far more powerful than half the world's nation-states, would seem to mock all he ever wrote and did. The capacity of "particular propriety" to enslave millions and degrade the very earth which he longed to see as a common treasury would surely convince him that, Reason or no Reason, the Lamb had finally been consumed by the Dragon. But walk on beyond the city, perhaps across the river into Buckinghamshire where "light" had shone in his own time, and he might begin to see something else. The land around him is still privately owned, and those who work and live on it are still divided into haves and have-nots. But something has changed. An Englishman's home and estate is no longer his and his alone. Over the past three centuries, and particularly the last one and a half, we have begun to understand and accept that the wider *community* has a *common stake* in the land, including private land. Land use is regulated by the *community*, by the conversations of democracy. The Parson Platts of this world, though they hold the title deeds, can no longer do whatever they like with it. Rambling members of the *community* have rights (albeit limited ones) to walk it, elected members of the *community* have planning powers over it, the national *community* even has powers to compulsorily purchase it for the public good, and the European *community* determines our land use to a degree unimaginable only a generation ago. The *community* now regulates what is still out of habit called private property.

An example: I "own" 25 acres of grassland in the Yorkshire Dales. I "own" it because I paid the market price to "buy" it from the previous "owner". It is legally *mine*. So I can do with it what I like? I cannot. It is subject to detailed planning restrictions. I cannot build on it, change any building on it, or change its use, without the permission of the local community, which in my case means the parish council, the county council and the Yorkshire Dales National Park. It is the community, not I, which determines whether a strip is taken for road-widening, a field for housing, another for a wild-life sanctuary. Members of the public have a statutory *right* to walk the designated public footpath through my meadows, farmyard and pasture. The community, in the form of the Ministry of Agriculture, Food and Fisheries, in alliance with the community of the European Union, determines the date on which I am allowed to cut my hay, the types and amounts of fertilisers I may use, and the numbers of sheep I may graze. And if I choose to run "my" farmland as an Environmentally Sensitive Area or a Site of Special Scientific Interest, it is with the community in the form of MAFF or English Heritage that I contract to manage "my" land in the way the community prescribes.

I hope no-one will suppose that I am so foolish as to argue that the struggle to make the earth a common treasury is won, or that Winstanley's revolution has arrived by stealth! Private and public rights in most places, and particularly on the vast estates of the Scottish Highlands, to cite a continuing cause of scandal, remain grotesquely out of balance. Movements like "The Land is Ours" (which has made Winstanley its patron saint) crusade for a fairer, more equitable balance *in the common interest*. But we would be blind not to recognise that privately-owned land in today's England is subject to far greater public control and regulation than it was in the Diggers' day. This is one result of the achievement of the democratic franchise for which the Levellers campaigned. The democratic franchise which Levellers and True Levellers demanded, and which was wrenched inch by inch from the grip of property over the succeeding three centuries, brought a diffusion of power, and the diffusion of power elevated *common* interest to a degree that would have had Parson Platt spinning in his privately-owned burial plot. That the diffusion remains uneven, that we must always be alert to the power-plays within our community politics, endlessly critiquing them in the conversation with ourselves that *is* democracy in action, is obvious to all of us. This is how we change things. This is how things have changed. And if we still have critical choices to make between the social and the free market, between paternalism and empowerment, between concentration and dispersal of the property/wealth/power axis, the long radical tradition with its many heroic failures and occasional glorious successes encourage us to stay in the struggle.

We are not obliged, then, to see Winstanley's story as one of what I earlier called "failure" in quote-marks. In his enduring words and his heroic deeds, he has fed our dreams, and our dreams drive us on to search out new ways of living in community, balancing necessary competition with co-operation, private with public interest, the personal with the general. That way we find new socialisms, new mechanisms for community and fellowship. And if, time and time again, what springs from our dreams proves flawed and inadequate, we dream on. When hope is killed, it is our dreams which ensure that new hope springs eternal. When the dream itself cracks, as Michael Tippett reminds us, we remake it and reshape it.

So when, today, we look at Georges Hill and see not rows of beans and barley sowed in common for common consumption, but an exclusive housing estate built by millionaire speculators for millionaire occupants, secluded from common society by burglar alarms, security patrols and "keep out" notices, we need not imagine that we are looking at the proof of Winstanley's failure. Rather should these and other monuments to "particular propriety" in its most banal form serve to stimulate the renewal of enabling dreams, from which spring the action which *is* "the life of all": action to ensure that "the land *is* ours", that the earth *is* our common treasury, and that the conservation of its resources *is* our common responsibility. That way we keep faith with Gerrard Winstanley and the Diggers all.

Notes

Chapter 1: The making of a revolutionary

1. G E Aylmer, introduction to *Englands Spirit Unfoulded* in *Past & Present*, No 40, 1968.
2. Winstanley's works are variously counted as 18, 19 or 20. Sabine's *Works* (1965) reprints or abstracts 19, including the *Letter Taken at Wellingborough*, which was clearly never intended to be published, but excludes *Englands Spirit Unfoulded* which was not discovered till later. The figure of 20 includes both of these but excludes those works noted by Sabine as "other works connected with the Diggers", in some of which Winstanley probably had a hand.
3. Information from the librarians at Wigan public library.
4. Lecture, *Winstanley: What do we know of his life?* at the Winstanley memorial conference celebrating the Diggers at St George's Hill, held at Brooklands College, Weybridge, April 9-10 1999, organised by Andrew Bradstock.
5. *Truth Lifting up its Head.*

Chapter 2: The "sea of truth" and the radical underground

1. A L Morton, *The World of the Ranters*, Lawrence & Wishart (paperback ed. 1979) p 106.
2. I am indebted to Sue Bell for this Rolle reference in an unpublished paper.
3. Andrew Bradstock, *Faith in the Revolution*, SPCK 1997, p 9.
4. Bradstock, *ibid*, p 27.
5. Christopher Hill,*The World Turned Upside Down*, Temple Smith 1972, p 22.
6. Christopher W Marsh, *The Family of Love in English Society, 1550-1630*, CUP 1994, p 260, citing *The Diary of John Evelyn*, ed. de Beer, p 868.

Chapter 4: "The vision

1. Christopher Hill, *"The Religion of Gerrard Winstanley"*, *Past & Present* Supplement No. 5, 1978, p 21.

Chapter 5: Action

1. *A Perfect Diurnall of Some Passages in Parliament*, No. 298 (April 16-23 1649), cited in *Making the News*, ed. Joad Raymond, Windrush 1993, p 392.
2. Cited in *Making News* (see above), p 394.

Chapter 6: Levellers Old and New

1. *Englands Moderate Messenger*, May 28- June 4 1649, cited in Brian Manning, *1649: The Crisis of the English Revolution*, Bookmark 1992, p 122.
2. *A Letter to the Lord Fairfax.*
3. Sabine, *op cit*, p 641.

Chapter 7: The Lamb's war

1. Sabine, *op cit*, p 320.
2. Sabine, *op cit*, p 17.

Chapter 9: The Rant

1. See Hill, *The World Turned Upside Down* as cited, p 173, and A L Morton, *op cit*, p 134.
2. Aylmer, *op cit* (note 1 to chapter 1).
3. Aylmer, *op cit*.

Chapter 10: The rout

1. Sabine, *op cit*, p 641.

Chapter 11: Mission to the churches

1. Lecture, *"If thou dost not act, thou dost nothing": Winstanley and the literature of revolution*, at Winstanley conference (see note 4 to chapter 1).
2. Andrew Bradstock, *op cit*, p 73.
3. Christopher Hill, *Winstanley: "The Law of Freedom" and other Writings*, CUP 1973, p 32.
4. Hill, *ibid*, p 250.

Chapter 13: Variations on an enigma: Winstanley and the Quakers

1. Lecture, *Winstanley: What do we know of his life?* at Winstanley conference (see above).
2. David C Taylor, *Gerrard Winstanley in Elmbridge* (pamphlet), Elmbridge Borough Council, 1982.
3. Richard T Vann, *"From Radicalism to Quakerism: Gerrard Winstanley and Friends"*, in *Journal of Friends Historical Society* No 49, 1959-61.
4. David & Anthea Boulton, *In Fox's Footsteps*, Dales Historical Monographs 1998. See also David Boulton, *"The Quaker Military Alliance"* in *Friends Quarterly*, October 1997.
5. Alsop as cited in note 1, this chapter.

Index of names and places